Praise for *Cats in the Belfry*

'The most enchanting cat book ever'

Jilly Cooper

'A chaotic, hilarious and heart-wrenching love affair with this most characterful of feline breeds'

The People's Friend

'If you read *Cats in the Belfry* the first time round, be prepared to be enchanted all over again. If you haven't, then expect to laugh out loud, shed a few tears and be totally captivated by Doreen's stories of her playful and often naughty Siamese cats'

Your Cat **magazine**

'An invasion of mice prompted Tovey and her husband to acquire a cat – or rather for Sugieh to acquire them. A beautiful Siamese, Sugieh turned out to be a tempestuous, iron-willed prima donna who soon had her running circles around her. And that's before she had kittens! A funny and poignant reflection of life with a Siamese, that is full of cheer'

The Good Book Guide

'*Cats in the Belfry* will ring bells with anyone who's ever been charmed – or driven to distraction – by a feline'

The Weekly News

'A warm, witty and moving cat classic. A must for all cat lovers'

Living for Retirement

'Absolutely enchanting... I thoroughly recommend it... One of the few books which caused me to laugh out loud, and it sums up the Siamese character beautifully'

www.summerdown.co.uk

'Every so often, there comes along a book – or if you're lucky, books – which gladden the heart, cheer the soul and actually immerse the reader in the narrative. Such books are written by Doreen Tovey'

Cat World

THE
NEW BOY

DOREEN TOVEY

summersdale

THE NEW BOY

Elek Books edition published 1970
Bantam edition published 1994

This edition published 2006 by Summersdale Publishers Ltd.

Summersdale Publishers Ltd
46 West Street
Chichester
West Sussex
PO19 1RP
UK

www.summersdale.com

Printed and bound in Great Britain.

ISBN: 1-84024-517-4
ISBN: 978-1-84024-517-2

Also by Doreen Tovey:

Cats in the Belfry
Cats in May
Donkey Work
Life with Grandma
Raining Cats and Donkeys
Double Trouble
Making the Horse Laugh
The Coming of Saska
A Comfort of Cats
Roses Round the Door
Waiting in the Wings

ONE

There was nothing, that last summer, to warn us of the sadness that lay so short a while ahead.

True, Sheba had been ill the previous autumn. 'Kidney trouble' the Vet had diagnosed after examining her. And when he told us gently that she was now an elderly cat, that her kidneys were very much enlarged but that with treatment and careful diet we might, if we were lucky, have her with us for another year – we were numbed at the prospect of the future without her.

For thirteen years life in our West Country cottage had been dominated by a pair of Siamese cats: Sheba, the clever one; tiny, blue-pointed and as fragile as a flower: Solomon, her noisy brother; seal-pointed, huge, our bumble-footed clown.

Every inch of the place held a memory of them doing something. Sheba playing tag with us on the coalhouse roof on a summer's night, for instance. Hanging over the edge bawling she was Here, we weren't to go in without her or the Foxes might Get Her – and then, as we reached up to lift her down, retreating light-heartedly to another corner saying Ha! ha! That one fooled us, didn't it? She wasn't afraid of Foxes…

Or Solomon, dark-backed and seemingly as unmoving as a doorstop, peering stolidly through the gate when he knew we were keeping an eye on him. Always the adventurer was Solomon. Never within our boundaries if he could help it and, on the occasions when we had to go out and were watching him like security guards to make sure he didn't get away (wipe a plate – out to check on him; put away a jug – out to check on him again), there he'd be sitting by the gate. Very ostentatiously With Us. Not a thought in his head about moving. Why on Earth, enquired the set of his back view, were we watching him Like That? And waiting, as well we knew, to vanish like Siamese lightning the moment we took our eyes off him.

One day, of course, we would have to lose them. The one disservice animals render us is that they don't live as long as we do. But cats live longer than dogs. We'd heard of Siamese of twenty and more. And not only had our two, until Sheba's illness, gone through life with the enthusiasm of eternal kittens, but it seemed such a little while since they *had* been young.

I could reach out, it seemed, and almost touch them like it. Going down the lane at three months old with their mother and their brothers in the wheelbarrow ... all the others in the wheelbarrow that is, and Solomon tagging tearfully along behind. Lying on our bed at six months old, when

Sheba had recently been spayed and, when we switched on the light wondering at the peculiar snicking noises, there was Solomon, mortified at being discovered, helping her by trying to bite her stitches out. The first time we took them to the Siamese cattery at Halstock after their mother had died and, as we left, they'd sat side by side in their big paved run, wistfully watching us go. They had the tips of their tails crossed, like children holding hands to give each other courage. They'd done that, said Mrs Francis, every time they sat out in their run.

Thirteen years had slipped by since then like May mist blown by the wind. The cats were seven when we acquired an eleven months' old donkey and now Annabel was seven herself. As wayward as ever and there was no need to worry about *her* age, thank goodness. Donkeys live to twenty at least, and we had been told they could live to forty.

I worried about the cats, though. Being the world's worst pessimist I always had done. I worried when they were ill. I worried when they were out of sight. When Solomon was out of sight, at any rate, for Sheba very rarely strayed. I ran like a deer at the sound of a cat-fight, in case the loudest, most urgent of the howls should be (as they usually were) Solomon, having started the fracas, bawling for me to come to the rescue. Sometimes I ran when it wasn't a cat-fight – bursting through the door, shouting 'SOLOMON!' as I went, only to find that it was the boy who lived on the hill practising bird-calls, or visitors to the Valley calling their dogs.

Embarrassing though it was, it didn't really bother me. I would have gone to the ends of the earth to rescue Solomon. To rescue any of them, if it came to that – but particularly

Solomon, who was not only more likely to *be* at the ends of the earth than any of the others, but because for me he was something very special.

I had never, for a moment, taken him for granted. In thirteen years I had never once seen him come round a corner or into a room with that dawdling, elegant walk of his, without marvelling at the perfection of his beauty. He had the proud, high-boned features of the East from which he came. His face shone like dusky silk. And if his slanted, sapphire eyes had faded a little with the years, they were the most loving, communicative eyes I have ever encountered in a cat.

Beyond all that, he was my friend. If Charles went down first in the morning it was Solomon who came flying up the stairs, stropping an exuberant strop on the stair-carpet by way of exercise and then, if I didn't acknowledge his presence, bumping his head against the door edge until I did and raising his tail in affectionate greeting. Sheba, who was Charles's friend, would be out with him inspecting the garden, but Solomon would wait while I dressed, walk down with me, and only then go out.

If I were missing of an evening – washing my hair, perhaps, and then drying it in the bedroom – it would be only a little while before there was a creak as he pawed back the heavy living-room door, or, if it were latched, the sound of his demanding that Charles should open it, and up he'd come again. His face bright with joy because he'd found me – and wasn't it Nice, his expression demanded, to be, he and I, together?

It was indeed, but sometimes I thought with a pang of the future. Nineteen or twenty, we told ourselves, but already

10

he and Sheba were thirteen. What grief was I storing up for myself when we lost him and what would I do when it happened?

In the event, however, it seemed it was Sheba who was going to leave us and if Solomon was my Number One cat, Sheba, as I'd so often assured her, was my Point Nine Nine Nine Nine. It was heart-rending, watching her sitting about so wanly while Solomon, doing his level best to get her going again, tore round the place like a spider-legged puppy. He shouted, he poked her with his paw, he invited her to chase him. She was Ill, she informed him mournfully. Couldn't he stop making such a racket?

She grew terribly thin and refused to eat. The Vet gave her treatment and said we shouldn't feed her proteins. They were a cat's natural diet, he said, but hard on the kidneys. When young, a cat thrived on meat and fish. When old, it did better on the cheaper tinned cat foods – and the more cereals they contained, in her condition, the better.

We tried six kinds of cat food but Sheba wouldn't look at them. So, despairingly – deciding that the most important thing at the moment was to get her to eat *something,* we'd worry about the cereal business later – we returned to the foods she normally liked. Dropped (knowing their habits of old when convalescent) in odd, seemingly accidental fragments in front of her, in any place where she happened to be sitting.

It was a long time before it worked. It was Solomon at first who ate the bits, nose to the trail like a walrus-whiskered bloodhound. Jolly good game this, he informed us enthusiastically. Got any more chicken scraps we wanted tracked down? But we got her eating in the end, on rabbit jelly. Dropped, I regret to say, on the seat of a chair.

Cats have these fads about feeding when they're convalescent. Solomon once, after a serious illness, consented to take nourishment only in the conservatory, from the toe of Charles's shoe. Crab paste it was, I remember, and Charles swore that his shoes reeked for weeks. Another cat I knew fancied shrimps in the bath as a pick-me-up. An empty bath, of course; he wasn't that psychiatric. But nobody was allowed to watch him while he ate; the shrimps had to appear before him one by one or the sight of them put him off; and his owners – I saw them myself – spent hours crouched low beneath the bath-rim, tossing shrimps to him over the top.

If anyone says how typically English that is and it just shows what fools we are about animals, may I also quote an American friend of mine, a hard-headed writer of detective fiction, who once spent the best part of a week on her stomach? Her cat, Robin, was convalescent, and would only eat best minced steak under her bed.

One book we read, discussing this finickiness, suggested dropping the food on pieces of paper. Humour them, it said. Try anything to get them interested. Often, when they're ill, they won't eat from dishes, but they'll take food put on paper because it's unusual.

Sheba wouldn't. On the chair, she informed us faintly. The one behind the door. It was the only place she felt like it – and if we didn't hurry up, the feeling would go off. So on the chair it was. And, as I'd recently re-covered the seat in tomato-coloured whipcord, an encouraging little spectacle it was, too, until I had the idea of slipping a spare piece of material deftly in front of her and feeding the invalid off that. The identical tomato-coloured whipcord, of course, so she thought she was using the chair. When I tried a piece of towelling she looked reproachful and once more refused to eat.

So, on rabbit jelly mixed with glucose, Sheba slowly turned the corner. A more repulsive mixture one couldn't imagine. It was sticky and looked exactly like sicked-up sherbet. But from that she went on to the rabbit itself and from rabbit to raw minced beef. And then, one day, quite by accident, I discovered about pigs' hearts.

By accident indeed, for I thought I was buying sheep's hearts. I spotted them in a butcher's in town, thought they might tempt our invalid, and in I went. 'Sheep's hearts? Certainly!' said the butcher, clapping a couple of gory objects on to a piece of greaseproof paper…

Sheba thought they were wonderful. She ate them with more relish than she'd eaten for years. She began to appear in the kitchen demanding them noisily. She sat around looking hopeful if I so much as got out the mincing machine. And then, after she and Solomon had been eating them for months – two a week between them and they polished them off like wildfire – I went into the shop one day, said I'd have a couple of those sheep's hearts in the window, and the new young woman assistant said 'But those aren't sheep; they're *pigs*!'

They were too, which shows how much of a Fanny Craddock I am.

'A' course I said they were sheep,' said the butcher when I taxed him with it. 'I says they'm whatever anybody asks for.

Saves disappointing people, to my way of thinking. Most of
'em can't tell pig from sheep or calf.'

Solomon and Sheba could. Switched precipitately to
lambs' hearts – pork, we'd always understood was bad
for them, and here they'd been eating pigs' hearts, raw,
for *months* – they promptly went on strike. Horrible old
Grey Fatty Things, grumbled Solomon, shaking his leg
disgustedly at his dish. Just when she was getting Better,
said Sheba, turning fraillly away from hers.

So, after consulting an expert on cat dietetics who said
there was nothing against pigs' hearts in his opinion –
nothing particularly in favour of them either, unless it was
that pigs were often given antibiotics, some of it probably
permeated into the heart tissues, and in eating the hearts
the cats might themselves be getting minor doses of the
antibiotic – we went back to them again. Only two a week
of course, along with fish and rabbit and meat. But our
cats liked and thrived on them. Robin, in America, liked
and thrived on them too. We gave up bothering about
Sheba's cereal. The Vet was right about it in principle, said
the expert, but, with an old cat, wasn't it better to let her
eat what she enjoyed? Rather a shorter life by a couple of
months or so than an existence on food she didn't like...
So, watching her closely, we continued. By Christmas she
was putting on weight. By spring she was back to hunting.
By autumn – a year from the time she'd been so ill – she
looked right for twenty or more.

Heartbreak was not far away from us, however. It was
Solomon who died.

TWO

We had no inkling whatsoever. Sometimes he drank more water than usual and I worried about his kidneys – but he always *had* done everything lustily. Big drinks when he drank. (Siamese drink lots of water anyway.) Hearty meals when he ate. Charging like a bull in a china shop when he felt like a chase around the house.

We watched him, nevertheless. Perhaps a *little* kidney trouble, we told ourselves, but if so he'd had it for years. We couldn't remember a time when he hadn't, after an afternoon's snooze in the car, come down, stood on the rim of the goldfish pond, and lapped a long and noisy drink you could hear the length of the garden away. But he wasn't *always* drinking, like Sheba when she was ill. Most cats get kidney trouble anyway as they get older, and so long as it stays slight it doesn't harm them.

So we reasoned, and gave thanks for his seemingly boisterous health. He was heavy; his coat was sleek; he looked and acted like a cat who was many years younger.

I have so many memories of Solomon those last few months. In the garden one day in spring, for instance, when it appeared that he wanted to dig a hole. The ground was hard – Charles and I not being very hoe-minded – so to help him I pulled out a dahlia cane and scratched the earth loose with that. Did Solomon get the message? Not the one I was intending, anyway. He spied suspiciously down the hole in case it held a mouse.

There was the time, too, when he actually caught a mouse. Charles had taken up bee-keeping. The combination of two cats, a donkey, Charles and a hive of bees had to be experienced to be believed and of that I will tell more anon. Suffice it for the moment to say that bee-keeping is not as easy as is sometimes thought, we were always having crises and having to send for a bee expert, and this was one of the times.

Charles had lost two swarms in a fortnight. Soon, he kept expostulating, he wouldn't have any bees at all. As far as I was concerned that would have been a jolly good job, but there we were. The expert expected momentarily, Charles in the garden waiting for him and Solomon mousing hopefully on the lawn.

He'd been sitting there on and off for weeks, in front of a clump of grass that grew over by the wall. He sat there when it was fine. He sat there when it rained. When it did, for fear of a chill on his liver I took out a wooden box, turned it on its side and in that, to the obvious surprise of callers, he sat imperturbably before the grass clump like a sentry at Buckingham Palace. It didn't seem odd to Solomon. That was just when one might come out, he said.

One hadn't. Or if it had, he hadn't seen it. No mighty hunter was Solomon, though he tried so hard to make believe he was. And then, the very moment the bee expert arrived, he landed one. A whacking great grandfather of a field mouse that probably couldn't get away, it was so fat. He lugged it to the middle of the lawn, eyed us forbiddingly over the top of it and prepared to defend it against the world. Make believe again, as well we knew. But through the gate right then came the bee expert, who was also a fervent animal lover – and the first picture he had of us – also animal lovers and pillars of the RSPCA to boot – was of a fierce, slit-eyed Siamese about to torture a mouse, and ourselves standing, apparently unheeding, by.

'Don't you take it away from him?' he demanded. We did, I explained, if it was alive. But this one looked dead – we were watching in fact, to see if it moved – and if it wasn't dead, its rescue needed strategy.

'On account of the cat's so fierce?' asked the bee expert.

On account, I explained, of the fact that we had for years been rescuing mice from Solomon by lifting him by the scruff of his neck – gently, so that, while his body and forepaws were in the air, his back legs were still on the ground – and that made him drop the mouse and then we caught it. But Solomon had now got wise to that one. When we lifted him he held his front paws out to catch the quarry himself if it fell – and, as a further precaution, bit deliberately through its backbone the moment we touched him.

'It would be dead then in any case,' I explained. 'So now we wait, see if it moves – and if it does and he lets go, we grab him before he can pick it up again.'

Solomon, as if to demonstrate, laid the mouse carefully on the lawn and looked at us.

'There you are, you see. Dead,' I said placatingly. At which the mouse got up and walked away. We would have saved it even then but for the fact that, as we moved forward to pick up Solomon, the bee expert advanced as well. Solomon grabbed the mouse and eyed us direly. Playing dramatically up to the role of a Panther Retreating With His Quarry (always the Walter Mitty was Solomon) he slunk, looking suspiciously over his shoulder at us at every step, to the corner of the cottage. And there – as, in an attempt to show the bee expert that we weren't as black as Solomon was painting us, I threw caution to the winds and chased after him – Solomon, of course, killed it.

That was bad enough. What was worse was that when the expert and Charles went off to the hive at the top of the orchard Solomon was tossing the dead mouse in an ecstatic Siamese ballet dance on the right hand side of the lawn. And when they came back again with their mission accomplished there was Solomon tossing another one on the left. It was no good pretending it was the same one, either. The first one had been big and fat and a field mouse. The second was a tiny pygmy shrew. Not only had Solomon, the world's biggest duffer when it came to mousing, managed for the first and only time to catch two in ten minutes, as Charles said starkly afterwards, he'd had to do it in front of someone who liked Nature so much, he wouldn't even wear gloves when handling bees. (If they stung him on his hands they might get away with it, he'd told Charles very seriously. If they stung into leather gloves, they'd lose their stings and die.)

So there we were. Solomon mousing, tormenting Sheba, going for walks... It was only a few weeks before he died that the Valley was flooded, and there was no sign of anything wrong with him then.

It began with a terrible thunderstorm. Our cats, following our own example, took no notice of it – but up on the hill Miss Wellington, as well we knew, would be heading for her broom-cupboard, cats and all. I tried to ring her up to comfort her, but there was no answer.

'Daft old besom' said our neighbour, Father Adams, when he called with a sack over his shoulder and a gift of cabbages and I told him about it. 'She takes the damned thing off the hook in case it gets struck.' I noticed him turn up the hill when he left our gate, nevertheless. Going up to be rude to her, no doubt – and to make sure, himself, that she was all right.

Meanwhile we put Annabel into her stable across the lane... Annabel, who takes good care of herself, poses like Love Locked Out on the hillside behind the cottage the moment it rains, and then stands there and drips disconsolately till we take pity and put her in... We lit a fire because, July or not, it was cold and the sight of it was bright and cheerful. And then we went upstairs to watch the storm.

We get tremendous storms over our West Country hills and this was no exception. The rain fell in a drumming curtain. The thunder growled around the sky like a prowling lion. Lightning flashed like scimitars around the horned Celtic camp on the hill beyond us. Solomon sat in the spare-room window with us, I remember, and regarded it all with interest.

It was Charles who first looked down and saw water coming under the gate. 'The bridge must be blocked again,' he said. 'We'd better go down and clear it.' The entrance to the cottage is over a bridge across the stream – a very small bridge under which sticks and leaves sometimes lodge and cause the stream to overflow. That wasn't the trouble this time, however. By the time we got downstairs the water was fanning silently across the garden like a tide coming in over sand, and, when we looked over the front gate, the stream was a rapidly rising river that filled the lane from side to side.

Things happened quickly after that. We ran for corrugated iron sheets – spare roofing for Annabel's shed – to barricade the gateway. But even as we got the front gate blocked the water came through the drive gate, higher up the lane, and poured in a wide red waterfall over the terrace wall.

Our first thought then was for the fishpool, down in the lower yard, which would be flushed out like a saucer under a tap by the surging force of the flood. 'The paving stones!' yelled Charles, inspired. We'd just had a load delivered to finish making the driveway. And so – we couldn't stop the water reaching the fishpool, we knew, but we hoped we might break the force of it and prevent the fish from being swept away – there we were, calf-deep by now in muddy water, frantically standing paving stones on end around the pool when Mr Penny came wading up the lane.

We must have looked queer to him but he looked pretty queer to us, too, paddling debonairly along with his trousers rolled up and a big black umbrella over his shoulders. His wife was out visiting up on the hill, he said. He was going up to tell her not to bring the car home. Five minutes later and he wouldn't have paddled up that lane. The stream, with water pouring down from the hills in all directions, was now a raging torrent, with boulders bouncing down in it like ping pong balls. For the first time we began to be worried. Was this really happening to us? And what could we do now that it was?

Too late, we realised we were cut off from Annabel. Between us and her stable, on the other side of the lane, now roared a fast-moving conveyor belt of angry red water and bounding rocks. Not only could we not have stepped into it without being swept away, but – if we had, by some miracle, kept on our feet and avoided being hit – we certainly couldn't have brought Annabel back with us. She would have panicked and probably drowned us all.

Feverishly we worked out two plans of campaign. The one for Annabel was that, if the water rose any higher, we would rope ourselves on a long line to the back gate, get across the torrent as best we could and hope to dodge the boulders, knock out the side of her stable and get her to the high ground behind it for safety. To that end Charles got the rope from the garage while he could still get the doors open, carried it wherever he went, and I, floundering behind him in waterlogged gumboots, tripped over it regularly all night.

The plan for ourselves and the cats was that we'd retreat, if necessary, to our bedroom, put Solomon and Sheba into canvas hold-alls (their baskets were already marooned in the tool-shed, with the door unopenable against the water) climb out through the side window onto the conservatory roof, and thence to the hill behind the cottage. We and the cats would be on one hill and Annabel on another, like goats on opposite Alps, but at least we'd be reasonably safe. Always supposing we could get back through the torrent from Annabel, and the glass held in the conservatory roof...

Fortunately it didn't come to that. The telephone went out of order. Lightning hit a transformer near the cottage and the Valley was plunged into darkness. The water went on rising until, in the kitchen, which is raised some way above the yard, it lapped ominously, like a high tide round a pier, at the top of the last retaining step... Solomon came out just then, surveyed the candlelit scene from the top of the step and held forth with indignation about this stuff which was in Our Kitchen... Another inch and it'd be in the Refrigerator, he complained; and what were we going to do about the Food? Then he went back, no more concerned than that, to join Sheba in front of the fire and, almost as if he'd been Canute, the water began to go down.

It rose once more after that, as a barrier of stones gave way higher up the Valley, and we held our breath for a while. Then, once again, it subsided. There was still a fast-running torrent between us and Annabel's stable but it was a foot, now, below the level of her doorway; then eighteen inches; then two feet... At three in the morning, knowing she was safe, we went to bed. At six we were up again, to inspect the damage.

The first thing I did was to go up and call across to Annabel that we'd be over to her soon, now that it was daylight. There hadn't been a peep out of her through the night and we hadn't dared call her in case, hearing our voices, she'd tried to break out and come to us, and been swept away immediately in the darkness. But now, hearing and seeing me across Charybdis, she let go of her pent-up feelings. WoohoohoohooHOO! bawled Annabel, and never have I heard such relief in a donkey's voice. Why she'd kept so quiet we couldn't imagine. Probably thought the Martians were landing, suggested Charles. And, being Annabel, didn't want them to know where Annabel was.

To reach her we had to jump a chasm in the ground, in which a torrent still raced where the lane had been. Later it was discovered that the surface of the lane had given way beneath the onslaught of the water and that this had actually saved us. Instead of flooding any higher across the width of the Valley the water had carved, in some places five feet deep or more, down to the level at which water-pipes had been laid thirty years before and in this gargantuan channel had rushed headlong down the Valley. The lane surface lay spread like some vast moraine over fields and footpaths further down. It lies there still today. It proved cheaper, in the end, to bring in new quarry waste to re-fill the lane. And it took a week of work to do it, with a non-stop shuttle-service of lorries.

Meanwhile, that first day after the flood, all was excitement in the Valley. Fortunately everybody was safe and for the most part had kept the water out of their cottages. But the gardens were flat with mud; those cabbages that Father Adams had brought us were the last he was to grow that year.

Everybody, unable to get their cars out, stayed at home, and brushed and hosed. All except Charles and I, who were frantically looking for the goldfish.

THREE

'What be doing? Burying somebody?' enquired Father Adams as he splodged through the mud into our yard.

Well might he ask. Now that the water had subsided, the paving slabs, so hastily erected the night before, stood on end around the fishpool like so many tombstones. Our yard resembled nothing so much as an ancient churchyard uncovered by the sea, the effect being heightened by several inches of mud all over it, a partly dried high-tide line just below the top of the stones and inside the pond itself, a rectangle of thick red oozing mud in which Charles and I were delving with saucepans.

We were looking, we explained, for our goldfish. 'Thee's 'ont find any of they' said Father Adams decisively; proceeding, without wasting any more time, to give us a summary of the disaster as he had so far encompassed it. A horse killed by lightning at the top of the Valley; hundreds of cattle lost across the moors; people in neighbouring villages marooned in their bedrooms… 'Old Ma Wellington twitterin' the place down wantin' somebody to get the doctor to see to her nerves,' he concluded inconsequentially.

Miss Wellington, safe in her cream-washed cottage at the top of the hill, hadn't lost so much as a tile. Despite the precaution of taking it off its hook her phone had gone out of order with everybody else's, of course – which was just as well since she couldn't now badger the unfortunate doctor personally. But her paths were unspecked by mud. Of the assortment of gnomes, rabbits and spotted stone toadstools which so coyly decorated her lawn not one had been so much as moved an inch. She couldn't even complain about the tradesmen. We in the Valley were reduced, as we were in heavy snow, to collecting our bread from the top of the hill and having crates of milk dumped communally on the corner. Miss Wellington had none of that but she was carrying on, apparently, as if she were marooned on a desert island.

'Reckons the village ought to be evacuated in case the flood comes again tonight,' said Father Adams. 'Says it's a judgement from the Lord for our sins. Didn't like it when I asked her what *she'd* bin a-doin' we didn't know about,' he chuckled raucously.

Why the Lord should have taken it out on our goldfish was, as Charles remarked, presumably clear as crystal to Miss Wellington, if not to us… As a matter of fact, all was well, though.

Scooping the mud out with saucepans, tipping it out behind us as we worked… no point in carrying it out to the lane, said Charles, when the yard looked like the

Thames estuary with the tide out in any case... we were about a foot from the bottom when we spotted the first glint of a red-gold side in a saucepan. 'It's dead,' I said despondently. 'It's *not,*' said Charles. 'I saw it move.' And sure enough, as we slid the fish, its gills and mouth blocked solid with mud, into one of the buckets of water we had standing ready, it dropped like a stone towards the bottom, flapped a couple of times as if it could hardly believe it, rose in a cavorting spiral as it realised it was free – and then, with obviously heartfelt relief, spat a mouthful of mud and gravel out into the water. It was so comic, the disgusted spitting out of the mud, that we laughed. We felt even more triumphant when, having scooped right to the bottom of the pool, fourteen large goldfish and a tench were swirling happily in buckets and bowls around the yard. Every one of the goldfish was there, thanks to the paving stones. The only occupant missing was a tench, and as tench invariably stay at the bottom of the pool anyway (we'd put two in when we built the pool, to clean it, and had never seen them since), it was obvious that it hadn't been swept away; it must have died some other time from natural causes.

We were standing there taking a breather, preparatory to starting work on re-filling the pool and getting the mud off the yard, when Father Adams came by again – this time with a friend he was taking on a tour to see the damage. Having spoken to us once already he raised a forefinger in acknowledgement and plodded on past the gate. His friend, however, whom we had never seen before, took one look at us, standing there surrounded by buckets of celebrating goldfish and, when he thought he was out of earshot, put his head near Father Adams's and muttered 'Didst thee see *that*?'

Voices carry easily in the Valley. 'Thass nothing to what they gets up to sometimes,' came back the untroubled tones of Father Adams.

How true that was – though always through force of circumstance.

It wasn't our fault, for instance, that a week later we were haring up and down the Valley busily blocking up the ends of water-pipes. There were three stretches of these – a fifteen-foot length that carried the stream under our drive entrance; a stretch of about thirty yards further up the Valley where the water had been piped past a field; and another length under the drive of a new house further on again. Normally the stream ran through them, high in the winter, low in the summer, gushing its clear, cold course down from the hills. But, as sometimes happens in limestone country, the force of the recent flood had opened up various swallets – swallow holes as they are sometimes called – in the stream bed. And down these fissures, until stones should accumulate and block them up again, the stream was now disappearing.

It seemed strange, after the roaring torrent of the previous week, to hear nothing but the buzz of the insects. The Council workmen had come and gone, leaving the lane with a brand-new surface and informing us with great excitement of the adder they'd found in their tea-hut. 'Only up a day he were,' the foreman told us – 'he' being the canvas shelter they'd put on the side of the lane. 'An' when Bill went in to start the brew-up, there were thic gurt adder on the floor.'

It wasn't surprising. We do have adders in the Valley, to which end the Council put up a notice a few years back. 'ADDERS! IF BITTEN RING SO-AND-SO 4321', it reads. As Charles commented at the time, we must be tough if they have to warn the adders…

Some visitors come here for years and never see them, but they are around all right. Safe enough if one keeps away from stone walls and long grass in summer – but there'd been a pair, we knew, in the orchard and occasionally we saw one in the lane. I always thanked my stars the cats weren't about when we did so. Cats are supposed to be natural snake-killers. Sheba, I had no doubt, would be. But I always worried about Solomon.

One thing about the flood, I said to Charles – it would have cleared out all the adders. Rotten for anything, to be caught by the water in its hole, but at least now the Valley was safe…

That was where I was wrong. What actually happened was that the adders, warned by some premonitory sense, must have made for higher ground ahead of the flood. For a week or two afterwards we'd had hot dry weather, and then they began coming back to the damp of the Valley bottom. Only now, with no stream running through it, the Valley wasn't so very damp. Hence the one curled up in the shade of the tea-hut; the one Charles killed – reluctantly, but there were children and animals to be thought of – as it lay, perfectly camouflaged, in the grass by the side of the road; the one I saw vanishing, with the ominous zigzag pattern on its back, into one of the empty water-pipes in the lane…

Up the lane had always been a favourite walk of Solomon's and as soon as the surface was replaced we'd started going again. We carried Sheba, who was apt to wail about the stones Hurting her Feet, or she Wasn't Coming At All, if we gave her the option. But Solomon bounded joyously along behind us, stopping to sniff here, spray a spray to beat all other cats' there, galloping after that on his long black legs to catch us up and, when he got to the new house, rushing in to roll ecstatically on its porch.

We used to joke that we'd better buy the house, he loved the porch so much. Then we'd put Sheba down for the walk back and she, forgetting her Feet, would rush in and dart, shouting, round the back of the house, and Solomon would chase joyfully after her, and Charles would stand in the lane and say they shouldn't go *in* there, on somebody else's property, while I had the job of getting them out again...

All part of the routine that Siamese like so much and it didn't take long for Solomon, noticing the now empty water-pipes, to decide that they could be incorporated into the schedule. It was tentative at first. The wide-eyed peering in at one end and out again; the venturing a bit further; the first silent-in-case-the-bogeyman-got-him emergence at the other end of the pipe. After that, of course, there was nothing to it. He dashed for the pipes as soon as we neared them; rushed madly up and down inside like a galvanised tube-train; sometimes appeared, shouting at the far end; sometimes shot back out of the end he'd gone in at, in the hope of surprising Sheba peering down it to see where he was; sometimes he hid in the middle and wouldn't come out at all and we worried in case something might have got him.

A *fox* could hole up in those empty pipes, said Charles and when I said but there'd be a battle if he met up with a fox… Well, a weasel then, said Charles, refusing to be comforted. It was only after I'd seen the adder going into the pipe that we realised the worst danger, however. It would be damp inside still, said Charles. The adders would go up there to get what water there was…

So that was how I started going ahead on walks, blocking the ends of the water-pipes so that Solomon couldn't go up them. We knew the stream wouldn't start running again till the swallets filled up again, of course, and that, even if it did, it would filter through the brushwood. But other people walking through the Valley didn't. So, thinking they were helping, they unblocked the pipes as fast as I blocked them. Life was one long nightmare in case Solomon went up one and encountered an adder; many a time I grabbed him by his tail just as he was vanishing up a pipe like the White Rabbit… it was a great weight off our minds when the stream began to run again.

It just doesn't seem possible now, Solomon bounding around like that. We went on holiday a few weeks later. I can remember, when we came back, Solomon accompanying me joyously up and down the garden in the rain while I helped unpack the car… Solomon rolling on the lawn, full of exuberance at being home… Solomon, less than a fortnight before he died, leaping through the air to catch a ping-pong ball… He liked that sort of game, he said. Hadn't played it for a long time, had we?

We'd been home for about a month when we noticed he was drinking a lot more water. Not just longer draughts when he did drink, but coming back to his bowl again and

31

again. He went off his food, too – quite quickly. Yet he didn't appear to be ill.

To be on the safe side, we called the Vet. It was his kidney trouble stepping up a bit, we thought. Treatment like Sheba had had would probably clear it.

This time it didn't. The Vet told us afterwards that in Sheba's case her system had achieved its own compensation. She was getting by with a lessened kidney area, as human beings are known to do. Sooner or later the trouble would come again, though, he said, and eventually there'd be nothing he could do.

With Solomon, this state had already been reached. He must have compensated on previous occasions, without our knowing. The Vet came every day for four days. For four nights Charles and I stayed up with him. On the fourth day, my birthday, we thought that we had won. His breathing had become laboured the previous night and it had worried us, but, in the early hours of the morning, it suddenly calmed. There was recognition, too, in his eyes when he looked at us, and, when I called him, he lifted his head and turned it in my direction.

'Happy Birthday,' said Charles and I thought it was my happiest birthday ever.

During the day, however, the laboured breathing began again. He was in no pain, said the Vet when he came at lunch time, but he was afraid that he was dying. As a last resort he gave him cortisone, but it was all to no avail. At five next morning, with my arms around him, Solomon left us. And it still seemed impossible that it could have happened.

FOUR

We buried him in our wood. In the clearing opposite the cottage, where the daffodils bloom in springtime and where once, when he was young, we'd watched him leap through the air like a salmon in pursuit of a wildly clucking pheasant. We buried him in his basket through whose air-holes, as a kitten, he'd once got his head stuck on a journey to Halstock and I'd had to push it back. It had been his basket all his life. He lay so very still now in the bottom of it.

Then we went back to the cottage and Sheba and another problem. How was she going to react to his loss?

Not too badly, it seemed at first. She purred at us, talked to us, ate her food as if nothing had happened. That night, however, unable to settle with our thoughts in the cottage, we went out for a while to visit friends. We left Sheba with a hot-water bottle on our bed, in a nest of sweaters as we'd always done. In the old days when we'd come home there'd been a thump as we opened the back door – Solomon jumping preparatorily off the bed – the sound of strenuous stropping on the stairs and, when we opened the door into the hall, the pair of them waiting side by side to greet us. Never were they crying, unless it was to tell us to Hurry Up. This night, however, as we came down the path, we heard a sound inside that struck to our very hearts. Sheba was crying with loneliness in the darkness.

She cried again that night when we went to bed. She hadn't always slept with Solomon. He liked his armchair in the living room with a blanket and a hot-water bottle in it, but Sheba, if it was a warm night or she was cross with him or he wouldn't stop snoring, would go off on her own on the settee. She never slept with him if he was ill, either. She hadn't slept with him now for almost a week. Always, though, they'd been in the same room together and that must have given her comfort. Either that or she now thought he was up with us and she was being left out of things. Anyway, there she was, crying downstairs so that we could hear her. So Charles went down and brought her up.

For the next four weeks she slept on my shoulder every night. In the old days, if we had them up with us, Solomon had that place while Sheba lay beyond him in touchy acceptance, ready to leap from the bed at once and Be an Outcast if Solomon or I so much as moved an inch. Now she stretched in my arms, luxuriated, purred whenever I spoke to her. First Cat at Last, she said.

If that had been that, I don't know what we would have done. Always in our minds had been the thought that if we did lose one of the cats we'd get another immediately. A rumbustious seal-point male, we'd said, or a little blue-point queen... The place just wouldn't be right without a pair of them. But was that fair now, with Sheba happier at nights than she had ever been...? Except that she was so unhappy during the day...

For the first couple of days presumably she thought Solomon was out somewhere. Then, realising she hadn't seen him for a while, she began to search. She would pause when she was eating and look round for him. Under the table? Coming through the door? But he wasn't there. She would sit upright in front of the fire in the evenings and look over her shoulder. Why didn't he come and sit by her? her expression demanded. She couldn't understand it – he always *did*.

One of their favourite places had been on our bed in the nest of sweaters. If it was cold, if they thought we were going out or if they just happened to feel like it, somebody would appear in the bedroom while I was there and hopefully inspect the bed. Up – being a sucker – I'd go with a hot-water bottle; the two of them would follow along behind me; I'd make up the nest while they sat and watched me and there, side by side on the bottle like a pair of Trafalgar Square lions, they'd stay happily for hours.

Now only one little cat asked for a bottle – and, when I gave it to her, sat day after day only on her own half of it, leaving the other space for Solomon and looking towards the door for him to come. At other times, when the waiting and wondering grew too intolerable for her, she'd go off on her own and start to call him. That was the worst thing of all for us to listen to. The lonely, heartbroken moaning, because she was Looking and he Wouldn't Come.

One night she was crying upstairs and we went to fetch her. We couldn't find her at first. She was hiding behind the armchair in the spare room, as she'd done so often as a kitten, calling him to come and waiting to pounce on him when he did. It was so many years since they'd played at ambushes round that chair. She must have been missing him to the very depths of her being to have remembered it and hoped it might bring him back.

It was then that we finally decided to get a kitten. The other things we'd been pondering over… Sheba's liking for being our only cat at night… whether, at her age, she'd accept a kitten… whether, when it came to the point, we could accept one ourselves so soon after Solomon's death… we must take a chance on these. The main thing was to get her a companion. Otherwise we might lose her, too, of grief.

The Vet, when we consulted him, said it was the best thing we could do. So did the Francises, who are experts in the ways of Siamese. Miss Wellington; said she was sure it wouldn't work and she didn't' know how we *could*. With mixed feelings, and with Solomon's pedigree, we set out on the search.

We took his pedigree, and a photograph of him as a kitten, because we wanted one as nearly like him as possible. So many people had said we could never replace him. 'You'll get another one and love him,' they said from their own experience. 'Just as much, but in a *different* way. It will never be the same, of course. It never can be. There are never two characters alike.'

There were going to be two alike if I had anything to do with it. I didn't want a different character. I didn't want the things I'd loved in Solomon to become part of the past. I wanted a cat who'd be Solomon again for me. So identically that in time it would be impossible to tell the difference. If we found a kitten who looked like him, I reasoned... if possible one with the same family tree... then surely there was a chance of their being alike in their ways? Charles said 'Well, we could try.'

It was much more difficult than I'd thought. For one thing it was October now and there weren't many kittens about, since most breeders aim for the November cat shows and the Christmas market. And for another, it was fourteen years since we'd bred Solomon and fashions in Siamese had changed. They were breeding them smaller now, with tiny marten faces. Solomon wasn't at all like that. I was looking for a cat with big ears, big feet and spotted whiskers, I kept telling people. They looked at me as if I was mad.

We saw some intriguing households on our travels, anyway. There was one way out in the backwoods of Gloucestershire, for instance. Remote, up a cart-track – one could imagine an owner taking refuge up there on account of it being safe. On account of there being no neighbours to see her in her more berserk moments, too, we decided. This was obviously someone with experience of Siamese.

How much experience we realised when we got out of the car and saw the notice – 'Sorry, no more kittens' on the door-handle. We knocked in case she might know of another breeder, but there was no answer. Instead, an indignant-looking Siamese appeared in the window and glared at us and we could appreciate why the owner had gone out. 'Sold all my kittens and left me Without Any,' the mother informed us. 'Just wait till she gets Back.'

There were plenty of kittens at the next place we visited – and there was also Oscar. He had a faint look of Solomon about him, but he had a bulbous nose. His points were coppery, too, instead of the dark seal ones we were looking for. There was something attractive about him, all the same.

There is something about all Siamese, of course. Oscar, nose and all, was in the room to start with, warming himself in front of the electric fire. When the dining-room door was opened in walked Mum – fashionably small and with a pedigree that would have done credit to the Pharaohs. When the kitchen door opened, six gleefully squealing kittens hurtled in from that direction, making like circus tumblers for the electric fire. They climbed it, they poked paws at it, they hid behind it except for one who climbed the television set and sat on top. Mum – named Sophia – posed on her owner's knee. Oscar, who was the last one left over from a previous litter, bounded among the kittens like an overgrown Alsatian, matching his long-legged lollop to their little scuttlings. In a moment the room was alive with cream-coloured happiness. I wished we could have bought the lot.

The kittens were too young to leave their mother, though. Only six weeks old and they should have been at least ten. And Oscar was six *months* old – too big for Sheba, we decided. If he jumped on her he'd knock her flat and she'd never like him. Any kitten would grow up to be heavily exuberant, of course. But we ought to inure her gradually – as it were, from the shallow end. They all had those bulbous noses, too. It was like being in a picture gallery of Habsburgs. Even the tiniest, most fragile of the kittens viewed the world from behind a huge, dark-copper Habsburg nose.

It wouldn't do, we reluctantly decided. Even if Sheba took to Oscar (which we were pretty sure she wouldn't, though we liked him a lot ourselves)... Even if we waited a month for one of the younger kittens to be ready (which we didn't want to do) we could never, with a nose like that, imagine we were back with Solomon. He liked *Us,* said Oscar, sitting determinedly down in front of us. I liked him too, I said, picking him up and hugging him. I hoped he'd find a good home. I could have loved him. But always I would have remembered another cat...

So many places we visited, only to be disappointed. At one house we did see a cat who looked like Solomon so much so that my heart missed a beat when I saw him. Alas, he was an unwanted neuter the people had adopted. Their queen, who was in kitten, was one of the small ones.

A formerly unwanted neuter, I should have said. He'd belonged to some people who'd decided to emigrate and they'd advertised in the paper to give him away. Luckily the Pitmans, who loved Siamese, had applied for him. For all his former owners cared he could have gone to anybody. He'd loved them, though, that was the pity. Two days after the Pitmans adopted him he disappeared. The Pitmans guessed he must have made for his old home, but, when they enquired, his former owners said they hadn't seen him.

'Didn't *want* to see him,' said Mr Pitman angrily. 'All they were interested in was their blasted boat to Australia.'

So, when Sappho did turn up at his old home, having crossed main roads and a railway line and somehow forded a river, the people he'd walked twelve heartbreaking miles to see took him back to the Pitmans again, dumped him out into the pouring rain and drove away. That was what the Pitmans thought must have happened, anyway. It was the only way they could account for the fact that, three days after Sappho disappeared, they heard a cat crying in the garden and when they opened the door, there he was, soaking wet and with raw and bleeding paws. He might, as Mr Pitman said, have walked back to his first owners. But he'd have stayed around them, however much they didn't want him. He wouldn't have come back again.

He'd had pneumonia after that and by the time the Pitmans had pulled him through he didn't want to leave them. There was a dog there to boss around, and Samantha the Siamese queen, and a family who seemed as if they wanted him...

He ruled them now as if they'd always been his people. He lay there loftily in the best armchair looking at us just like Solomon, while they told us about his achievements. How he went to bed with them at night, for instance. Sleeping between her and her husband with his head on the pillow, said Mrs Pitman, while Samantha slept as good as gold in the airing cupboard.

One night her husband had gone on strike and said he wasn't going to have that cat in bed with him. (Not that he didn't *like* him, said Mrs Pitman, but Sappho took up so much room, they always ended lying on the edge.) Sappho, evading eviction, took refuge under the bed. It was no good trying to entice him out with rabbit. Sappho said firmly he didn't want it and he wasn't Coming. Until, said Mrs Pitman, her husband got out of bed to close the window, which he'd forgotten – when Sappho was out, up on the pillow and under the sheets in one fast black streak. You couldn't help laughing, said Mr Pitman admiringly. They couldn't turn him out, after that.

Sappho had landed in clover all right. You could tell that by the way, when the Pitmans' daughter brought him a saucer of milk, he condescended to drink it. On his side in the armchair, languidly lifting his head to lap. You could tell it, too, by the story of the time they'd lost him. He was such a one for going exploring around the neighbourhood, said Mrs Pitman; they never knew where he was going to turn up next.

Anyway, they'd been enquiring around for hours on this occasion when somebody said they'd seen him earlier in the Johnsons' farmyard, and when they got there, there was this great big heap of steaming manure which they knew hadn't been there that morning... They always thought the worst, she said resignedly. (I could understand it. After years of Siamese cat-keeping, so did we.) And the farmer wasn't there, to ask permission, and they dared not use spades, for fear of hitting Sappho with the edge...

So when the farmer came back, there they were, she and her husband and the children, frantically moving the manure heap with their hands. She and her daughter were crying, she said reminiscently, imagining poor little Sappho suffocated underneath.

'That gert dark-coloured cat? Oh, he were frightened by die tractor when I brought the muck in,' the farmer said heartily. 'Went up thic old tree. Han't he come back home then?'

Sappho in fact was still up the tree. Not twenty yards from the manure heap, and he'd been watching them from it all the time. Right at the top and he must have been shouting for help, before they came, for hours. When they fetched a ladder and got him down, he'd completely lost his voice.

Well, there we were. He and Samantha had settled down with one another. And he'd been four when they had him, while Samantha was two. It encouraged us to think that Sheba might be all right, too, when we got our new boy.

Only – were we *ever* going to find a kitten just like Solomon?

FIVE

They say it's always darkest just before the dawn and that Saturday night I'd just about given up hope. We'd rung every breeder we'd ever heard of, travelled all over our own and neighbouring counties and so far we'd drawn a complete blank. When the phone rang I almost didn't answer it. I was so tired of saying No, we hadn't found him yet.

It was someone ringing up with more addresses. Dutifully I thanked her, half-heartedly rang the numbers… It was the usual story. No kittens at the first place. Small ones at the second. (I always asked if the kittens were small and almost without exception the answer was Yes.) But the third… Oh no, hers weren't *small*, said the voice enthusiastically. She had the mother *and* the father, and the father was *huge*. Yes, *and* dark and with big bat ears… That was just like Orlando. She'd try to keep him in if I'd like to see him.

I hadn't heard amiss. Orlando, it seemed, wasn't kept penned like most pedigree stud cats. They had only one breeding queen themselves, explained Mrs S. They bred because they liked the kittens about the place, not as a business. So they had to let Orlando out to find other wives, or the place would never hold him.

It was only just holding him the following afternoon. We were standing in a hall that looked as if it had come straight out of a Hollywood film set. A luxurious, deep-pile carpet covered about half an acre of floor. In the centre an open-tread, wrought iron staircase swept in a striking curve towards the landing. On the right, in an alcove, was a pool in a rockery grotto, with concealed green underwater lighting and fish gliding lazily among the water lilies. I was still goggling at that... my mind registering *goldfish*... indoor *fishpool*... surely not with Siamese *cats*... when a flap opened in a door at the back of the hall and a Siamese kitten scurried through, gave us a sharp-eyed glance in passing and disappeared into a room on the left.

'That's one of them. One of the boys I think,' said Mrs S. 'And the one making the noise is Orlando. We've kept him in since breakfast and he doesn't like it.'

Noise was the understatement of the year. Orlando sounded as if he was being sawn in half. He wanted to Go Out. He'd promised to meet Another Cat. WANT HIM TO TEAR THE PLACE DOWN? roared a voice that had more than a hint of Solomon's in it. HE'D START ON IT PRETTY SOON, warned the voice after a much-needed pause for breath.

We went into the room. If one didn't know Siamese one would, from the uproar, have expected to see something approaching a sabre-toothed tiger and – if they were present at all and not hiding panic-stricken under a bed somewhere – a clutch of terrified kittens and a nervous, intimidated queen. We'd had experience, however. It was no surprise to us to see a trio of smudge-faced kittens tumbling unconcernedly over the furniture, a seal-point female cleaning her back leg on the hearth-rug, and none of them taking the slightest notice of the huge, black-shouldered male who, with his eyes shut tight to help him shout better, was sitting bawling to himself in the middle of the floor.

It was a room that matched the hall. Enormous, magnificently carpeted, a grand piano on one side and settees dotted about as if it were the Savoy. There were enough Siamese for the Savoy, too. Orlando, his wife, three kittens and – for the moment I thought I was seeing things – another huge seal-point and a blue-point as well. Mrs S., following my gaze, explained. The blue-point was their previous breeding queen, now enjoying a well-earned retirement. The seal-point, William, was one of Orlando's grown-up sons. Neutered of course, said Mrs S., or he wouldn't have got on with his father. With Orlando himself away so much, it was nice to have a boy around the place.

It wasn't the number I was staring at. It was the fact that there was not just one cat like Solomon regarding me from these ultimate-in-luxury surroundings, but – I could hardly believe it – *three*. Orlando and his wife, who were very much alike to look at. And, surveying us loftily from the lid of the grand piano, William, their neuter son. It was like looking at Solomon in a triple mirror. The same eyes, the same bone structure, the same velvety dark-seal colouring. It was hardly surprising, when we compared the pedigrees of Solomon and Orlando, to find that Solomon's father, Rikki, was on them both. A good way back as far as Orlando was concerned, of course. Rikki was his great-great-grandfather.

The only question now was which of the two male kittens we would have. The one who, having finished playing, was sitting Thinking, with his paws tucked under him in an armchair – or the one, long-legged, with gangling hindquarters, who was still jogging restlessly round the floor? As we watched, the jogging one went up, dabbed a paw at his father and challengingly put his ears back. That was the one, we said.

We brought him away with us. Something must have told us this was going to be the place and for the first time ever on these kitten-hunting expeditions we'd taken a basket with us. Sheba's basket In due course we'd get a new one for the kitten.

We'd brought an earth-box, too, because we were going to visit Charles's brother afterwards and had decided to take the kitten with us if we bought him. And – it could only happen to us, I thought – I was clutching a carrier bag half-filled with turkey legs.

It had been given to us by Mrs S.'s husband – to keep the kitten going till the shops opened, he said. No, they didn't buy it specially for the animals. It seemed they had a friend who ran a country club. Turkey figured regularly on the menu, when there was any left over it was given to them for the cats... the kittens had been practically raised on turkey and chicken, he said.

So there we were, driving along with an earth-box, a bag of turkey and, squalling his head off on my knee in Sheba's basket, the new boy. He'd looked very much like the photograph of Solomon as a kitten when we'd compared them. Big ears, huge paws, the same broad-browed, little black pansy face. Right now he was sounding like Solomon, too. Kidnapped! Claustrophobia! LET HIM OUT! It could have been Solomon en route to Halstock in that basket. The basket itself, too, in which Sheba had tranquilly sat, holding affable conversation with us through the airholes, on so many of her own journeys to Halstock was now giving a remarkable impression on my lap of a landmine about to explode at any moment.

'At any rate he doesn't stick his paws out,' I said, doing my best to lighten the atmosphere. (Somebody had to try to lighten it, anyway. Charles, hands gripped grimly on the wheel, was wincing as if a sledge-hammer was hitting him at every bellow.) I should have known better, all the same. The next moment a black-socked paw shot frantically through an air-hole and hooked Charles's coat-sleeve like a salmon gaff.

The kitten survived the journey to Charles's brother's house at any rate, which was one eventful milestone passed. Then we let him out of the basket in their sitting-room and I had something else to worry about. Big though he was for his age, he looked so very small and vulnerable sitting there alone. It was years since we'd had a kitten and there were so many dangers to protect him from. Adders... foxes... going up empty water pipes and getting lost out over the hills... And he'd been brought up in all that luxury... with an indoor goldfish pool... on *turkey*... How could we ever hope to raise him?

He wasn't worrying, that was obvious. He sat on everybody's lap, tried out the furniture for scratching, importantly spent a penny behind the settee when we showed him where we'd put his earthbox. Sit up, paws together and Show People his mother had evidently told him. And alone, very small, among strangers, he sat as tall as he could in his earthbox and performed with the dignity of a prince.

He didn't eat his food like one, unless it was Henry the Eighth. Even Solomon in his heyday hadn't guzzled as fast as that. Or had he, perhaps, and we'd forgotten? Anyway, he went through a plate of turkey like a steam shovel, drank several saucers of milk... Occasionally he looked up at his admiring audience and, with his mouth full, blissfully said 'Waaah!' And then, having sat for a while and warmed himself, he put himself to bed. His mother being nowhere in sight he selected, as the nearest thing he could find to her, Charles's brother who was wearing a large cream sailing sweater. Biggest Siamese he'd ever seen, said Seeley, curling like a small white snail on his chest.

Seeley was my name for him. Officially he was Solomon Secundus but I couldn't say 'Solomon' yet without remembering... So 'Seeley' I called him temporarily, as befitting a seal-point cat.

Gosh, he was a super little chap, said Charles as we drove back to the cottage that night. To be as brave as that among strangers. He certainly had what it took.

He remained a super little chap even when, from time to time on the homeward journey, he woke up and started to yell. 'He's only a baby and it's dark,' said Charles benevolently. 'Gosh, I shan't half be glad to get to bed.'

Famous last words again, of course. An hour later, far from being in bed, we were tearing up and down the lane with torches because Seeley had disappeared.

How it had happened we just couldn't think. Deciding to leave his introduction to Sheba until the next day (we'd have more strength then, said Charles; he had a feeling it was going to be a bit of an ordeal) we'd fed her up in our bedroom, him downstairs in the living room... we'd shut doors like Davey escape hatches to stop them meeting each other by accident... he was feeling really *giddy*, said Charles, remembering who was where... we'd made Seeley a bed with a hot-water bottle on the settee (Sheba was sleeping up with us)... we'd given Seeley a clean, fresh earthbox (and another one upstairs, of course, for Sheba)... If we really *had* finished shutting doors like Secret Service conspirators, said Charles, perhaps we could now go up to bed? With which I fetched the fireguard (the fireplace was empty but we didn't want the kitten going up the chimney); Charles brought in the key and bolted the door and when I went to show Seeley where his bed was, Seeley had completely disappeared.

We looked. Up the chimney, where Charles was sure he was because I hadn't put the guard up soon enough. In the garden, where I was sure he was because Charles had opened the door to get the key in. In the bedroom, where with a sudden thought we rushed concertedly in case he'd got up there with Sheba and she'd murdered him. Back down again to the garden because, as he wasn't in the house, he *must* have got out.

My imagination worked overtime as I scurried. Surely he couldn't be trying to walk home again, like Sappho, to *his* first owners? I had a heartrending vision of a tiny, brave white figure trudging determinedly along the roads. What would the people we'd bought him from say when we told them we'd lost him? I had an equally heartrending vision of myself (it wouldn't be Charles) having to ring them up and confess. Supposing a fox were to get him? I turned cold, and started to listen for the screams.

We'd have been hunting all night – flashing torches, frantically hurrying and shouting to scare off the foxes – if I hadn't, in case somehow we'd managed to miss him, gone indoors again.

Upstairs – no. Nor in the kitchen or the hall or in the bathroom. And the living-room was so completely silent. If he was there, I thought, I would have sensed it. It had been so full of his presence so short a while before.

It was full of him still, as a matter of fact. What made me look there I didn't know but there he was, curled up where – when, being such a little cat, he could stay up no longer – he'd put himself to bed. Under the table, on the seat of a dining chair. He was Sleepy, he said when I lifted him out. Not in the big, tearer-up-of-baskets voice that had deafened us in the car but with the tiny, beguiling mew of a very small seagull.

We were sleepy, too, but it was several hours before we got any. We'd wanted a kitten like Solomon and now we'd obviously got him. We had years of this ahead of us, said Charles, lying starkly on his pillow. Was he telling me, I replied, lying equally starkly on mine. My mind was a whirl of foxes, adders, passing cars, and – brought back clearly by this initial crisis over Seeley – the panic-stricken hours

I'd spent ranging the hills for Solomon when he, too, had vanished Siamese-fashion into thin air.

'I think I'll build a cage,' Charles announced after a while of heavy thinking. Not a small one, he explained, but a run – well, rather like a fruit cage. So we could put Seeley in it when we wanted to be sure where he was.

'What about the bees?' I said, having visioned up another danger. Seeley going up to a beehive and trying to look inside.

We planned the cage, discussed the bees, considered Annabel. Seeley mustn't be allowed to get into her field, said Charles: just imagine her hoof coming down on him… I hadn't got round to that one but I imagined it now, all right. Also on the agenda was putting covers on all the water-butts. And the foremost problem of all, of course – introducing him to Sheba.

It was morning before we slept. Sheba, not knowing what was coming to her, snuggled cosily on my shoulder. Eventually, not very sure of what was coming to us, either, though we imagined we'd covered all the immediate eventualities, we went to sleep too.

We got up at seven, unbolted the kitchen door, went out into the yard for a breath of country air before embarking on the trials of the day – and one eventuality we hadn't foreseen immediately presented itself. Seeley went out ahead of us and fell straight into the fishpond.

SIX

So there we were, once more towelling down a drip-
ping wet cat on the kitchen table. 'Just like Solomon,'
said Charles reminiscently. It was, too, except that
when Solomon had caused a commotion by falling in
the fishpool all those years before, he'd been chasing a
hare and had gone in at full gallop, while Seeley merely
toddled innocently across the yard, mounted the log
in front of the pool that had been one of Solomon's
stropping posts and, with his head turned firmly to
the left taking his first wide-eyed look at the lawn,
meanwhile continued in line ahead and simply plopped
straight in.

It was amazing how sometimes – as at the moment we'd
first seen him, for instance – he could look such a big
kitten with such long and gangling legs, while another time
– like going across the yard – he could look so very small.

Toddling was the only word for it, on those fat little black-socked paws.

If we'd thought Sheba was likely to be won over by his smallness, however, we were very much mistaken. We dried him off, gave him some breakfast, had some ourselves to give ourselves strength for the ordeal. Then, feeling something of a traitor now that the moment had come, I brought Sheba down from the bedroom. All those years with Solomon, I thought, and now how were we going to upset her?

She didn't attack him, as we were half afraid she might do. She simply gave him a haunted look, then turned and went back upstairs. She stayed up there all day, hunched pathetically on the bed. It wasn't her home any more, she informed us, when we tried to coax her down. We'd brought in another cat to supplant her. She was going to stay upstairs now and Die.

That brought home the passing of the years more clearly than anything. She and Solomon had been four when we'd previously tried to introduce a kitten to the cottage. As a playmate for Solomon the idea had been, because Sheba was already rather prissy and Solomon got bored at times. Sheba had soon put paid to that little plan. Boadicea leading the Iceni had had nothing on her campaign against Samson. She'd spat at him, sworn at him, spied on him sinisterly through windows... she'd had a fight with Solomon, too, and bitten him in the paw... Half a chance and he'd Like that Kitten, she screamed, pitching into poor old Fatso. And then she'd begun to spit at Charles and me and we'd had to take the kitten back... That was another reason we'd been apprehensive about having Seeley. With Solomon – yes, we'd have said it might have worked. But with Sheba, we still remembered Samson.

We hadn't expected this dispirited attitude, though. We brought her down once more. She was our very best girl, we assured her, stroking and making a fuss of her. She looked at Seeley with the expression of a defeated deer. She wished she was with Solomon, she said, as she crept upstairs again.

It was Seeley who broke the ice in the end and in that the Fates must have been with us. Had we chosen a kitten bred in the usual way – brought up by its mother in maternal seclusion; never having seen another adult cat; never realising there *were* such things as other cats – he would probably have been terrified of Sheba. In his case, however, he'd been brought up with three adult cats in permanent residence, a father who came and went in the style of a commuting stockbroker… Grown-up cats had no terrors for Seeley, who had learned long ago that their growls were worse than their bites and they would never hurt little kittens… well, so long as the little kitten didn't try his luck *too* far, anyway…

So when we brought Sheba down again, shutting the door this time so she couldn't creep back upstairs, and, finding herself unable to escape, she put her head down at him and did a sinister, slow-motion snarl that would have frightened the daylights out of a bull-moose, he simply hurled himself at her with squeals of delight and told her how pleased he was to see her. Gosh, she was Nice. He'd like her for his Friend. What was her Name? he was obviously asking.

From the expression on her face Sheba was equally obviously refusing to tell him. She ate little cats like him, she informed him threateningly. That was all she did, though. Threaten. And, since he refused to be intimidated, stage two of their introduction consisted of Sheba sitting round in attitudes of beleaguered desperation while Seeley, his face abeam with adulation, sat determinedly beside her.

He tried so hard to copy her, it was absolutely priceless. If Sheba sat upright, he – all eight important inches of him – sat upright too. If Sheba squatted on the corner of the table with her paws tucked resignedly under her – there beside her, imitating her as hard as he could go, squatted Seeley with *his* paws tucked under him. It was no good her retreating under the table, either, and hoping that that would show him how much she hated his company. Two shakes of a kitten's tail and he was under the table too. Nice under here, he said, sitting as close to her as he could get. Sort of cosy and secluded and being-in-a-cave-like, wasn't it?

It was beginning to have an effect on her. We could tell that when she gave up snarling at him and started the staccato chittering she used for putting the wind up birds. This was supposed to be extremely frightening, as she emphasised by stretching out her neck and flattening her ears at him, but we hadn't had her all these years for nothing. Our Sheba was beginning to waver.

Estimates had varied as to the time it would take them to become friendly… from four days to a fortnight to Miss Wellington's determined forecast of Never. They first met on a Monday morning. It was in fact exactly two days later, on Wednesday morning, that Seeley clambered determinedly up the stairs and into our bedroom where, having exhausted all other methods of shaking him off,

Sheba lay in the one place he hadn't yet followed her to – on our bed, in the nest of sweaters. He'd got as far as the landing the previous day and we'd hurriedly nipped him away again. This time, however, we let him get on with it. Over the ramparts of sweaters he tumbled, greeting Sheba with squeals of rapturous delight. So *that* was where she was... Gosh, it was nice in here... Wasn't she *clever,* to have found such a super place to sit in?

Sheba's ears were so flat she looked like a greyhound and our hands hovered ready to snatch the intrepid one to safety if she lashed out at him. What *could* she do with someone loving her as much as that, however? Seeley, with one flop of his fat little body, threw himself on the bottle beside her and licked her face, his eyes ecstatically closed. Sheba, her ears still flat, sat stiff as a ramrod while he did it and then, after a moment or two and obviously very much against her will, licked him grudgingly, very self-consciously, in return. And that was that. When I went up to check on them five minutes later he was asleep against her side while she – you could see the peace in her eyes – lay contentedly, with her head stretched out on another cat's flanks, for the first time in more than a month.

She didn't cry for Solomon after that. She was too busy keeping an eye on Seeley. It wasn't that she particularly liked him, mind you. She had accepted him, as she couldn't find Solomon, as one of her own kind who she could be with and watch as he moved around; who would introduce familiar cat noises into this suddenly wrongly-quiet household; who would do something to lessen the loneliness within her. Obviously, too, she tolerated him because he was a kitten. There wasn't any question of her doting on him, however. What she was busy coping with was Seeley's devotion to *her*.

His greatest ambition, it seemed, was to be Just Like His Friend Sheba. If she walked anywhere, he trotted enthusiastically alongside her. If she sat down, he sat down too. If she drank from her water-bowl, he rushed to have a drink himself. If she curled up on the hearthrug, so did he.

That was all very well, but when it came to following her to her earthbox, sitting bang in front of it and watching, while she performed, with an expression of rapt admiration on his face, it really was too much. Gosh, wasn't she Clever, said Seeley, his eyes as round as an owl's. Couldn't she have any privacy Anywhere? demanded Sheba, stepping stiff-legged and offended from the box.

We were a bit suspicious about his insistence on sharing her food with her, too. Given separate dishes he would gobble away at his like a steam shovel, shouting encouragingly as he ate that he was Coming, he wouldn't be a Minute. He would keep looking over at her longingly. He would run halfway to join her and then, pulled by the thought of what he'd left behind, rush back to his own dish again. Eventually – overcome, ostensibly, by his desire to be with her – he *would* leave his own plate and join her at hers. He would then, with his head thrust under her unprotesting nose, proceed to clear that at an even faster speed before returning, jet propelled, to finish his own.

In the end, yell though he might about he Loved Her and wanted to share his All with her, we had to feed them separately. Sheba in the kitchen, where she ate placidly, slowly and with a good many squawked asides to Charles (she always ate better when Charles was there); Seeley in the passage outside, where he whipped through his share as if he hadn't been fed for a month – after which there would be a noticeable silence which meant he was trying to look under the door. To make sure Sheba was there, he said when I caught him at it. To gauge the chances of Sheba leaving any was more like it in my opinion.

He ate fast. He drank fast – in such large quantities I worried, having such things still very much on my mind, about *his* kidneys, till Charles said there couldn't be much wrong with them at Seeley's age and it was undoubtedly all the shouting he did that made him thirsty. And he moved fast.

Not only horizontally but vertically, so that often, without even realising he was in the room, the first thing I knew about it he was galloping up me like a squirrel. Like Solomon, however, he couldn't climb for toffee. One initial bound and he was invariably left frantically swinging from something – in my case usually hooked well and truly to the seat of my pants. With Charles, who was taller, he only got as far as his knees. Charles's yells at such times were quite unearthly. When, in fact, on Seeley's second day with us, Charles came hobbling into the bathroom holding his knee and asking for the sticking plaster I was really quite impatient with him. Shouting like that, I said. Making all that fuss. Because a tiny little kitten had climbed his leg. 'You'd shout too,' said Charles 'if you didn't have anything on under *your* trousers.' And sure enough, under the single thickness of his trouser leg, poor old Charles's knee-cap was bleeding streams.

Poor Charles, he just couldn't win. He was sitting one night in an armchair reading, with Sheba on his knee. Seeley had been with us for about a week by this time and Sheba was slightly off her food. A bit overpowered by the boisterous Seeley, we'd decided; we must give her extra attention to boost her morale. Extra attention included coaxing her appetite, of course. So there was I, with Seeley banished temporarily to the kitchen, feeding Sheba with bits of pig's heart on Charles's knee. She ate a bit; fumbled a bit; ate a bit more. By the time she'd finished Seeley was howling blue murder at being locked in the kitchen, I was fishing bits of pig's heart from where they'd fallen down the side of the chair, and Charles was complaining loudly about his trousers. What he put up with for these damned cats, he said. His knees torn to ribbons, threads pulled on all of his clothes, and now pig's heart juice all over his trousers...

I'd soon take care of that, I said, fetching a cloth and a bowl of water from the kitchen and briskly setting to work on his trousers. It was all right, of course, until the dampness penetrated. It was a November night, the water from the tap was very cold and the moment it got through to Charles he nearly hit the ceiling. Goshdammit, he said. What was I trying to *do*? Freeze him solid? Even Seeley stopped shouting and listened, out in the kitchen.

The next thing that happened was that Sheba lost her voice. It followed her loss of appetite and we couldn't understand it. One day she was talking away confidingly to us in her usual cracked soprano – about we three were Friends, weren't we?... she was allowed out on her Own, wasn't she?... little kittens were very Silly, weren't they?... and Charles and I agreeing with every word – and the next, all that came out when she opened her mouth was a tiny, hard-to-get-out squeak.

It had never happened before in fourteen-and-a-half years. Perhaps it was delayed shock at losing Solomon, we decided – or subconscious resentment at our adoption of Seeley. Maybe all the chittering she'd done at him had strained her throat. Or was she perhaps jealous, and trying to sound like a baby herself?

We didn't call the Vet. She didn't appear to be ill and for the moment the thought of the Vet was synonymous with Solomon. After two days, in fact, her appetite came back – but not her voice. As the days went by and still she squeaked we began to think that it never would. And then, a fortnight after she'd so suddenly gone semi-mute, Charles said excitedly one morning, 'She spoke!' She did, too. With a vengeance. When I went out to ask her how she was feeling – 'WAAAAAH!' said Sheba profoundly, in deep contralto.

She'd been a soprano previously. Eventually her voice did become lighter again, though never so high-pitched as before. Something had damaged her vocal chords – and still we put it down to probable shock. Until, some weeks later, I happened to be having tea with Janet up the lane and she said that her cat, Rufus, had been off-colour. Wouldn't eat for days, she said, and then he had lost his voice. Not that he'd ever had much of one, but it had gone right away to a squeak.

Her theory was that Rufus had picked up a germ from a stray cat she'd seen hanging around. Sheba, sniffing the garden in search of Solomon before Seeley came, could similarly have picked it up. It hadn't occurred to us that it might be an infection of some sort – as, obviously, it undoubtedly was. As we'd have suspected, too, of course, if Seeley had also caught it.

Presumably Seeley hadn't caught it because, having just come from his mother, he was still well endowed with antibodies. He was meanwhile engaged in other ways of worrying us. Like trying to get up the chimney.

SEVEN

That was one of the very few ways in which he differed from Solomon. Solomon had never been the least bit interested in the chimney. Sheba had stood on her hind legs once and peered inquisitively up it – after which she'd decided a passing gnat was a lot more interesting so she'd chased that instead and left an ivy-leaf trail of artistic black pawprints all up the sitting-room wall. But other than that it meant nothing to them at all.

We put a guard over the fire when we went out, of course, and there were guards, for safety's sake, on all the electric fires. We had to watch those, I must admit, because Solomon was an expert at threading his tail through the cross-pieces. I remember, on one occasion, someone asking me on the phone how he and Sheba were. 'Fine,' I replied, never thinking to cross my fingers. 'Absolutely bounding. Not a single thing wrong with them for once.' And no sooner did I put down the phone and open the sitting-room door than Solomon, who was sitting in front of the fire, stood up, raised his tail, backed a step or two in his usual dance of greeting – and stuck his tail straight through the guard wires and onto the fire. It was all right. I whisked him away too fast for the heat to get to his skin. But there we were, not five seconds from saying how perfect everything was, with a horrible smell of singeing and Solomon's tail scorched in poker-work stripes that didn't grow out for weeks. It just doesn't pay to be complacent with Siamese cats.

We hadn't been complacent with Seeley. When, on his very first day with us, we found him clinging like a little white starfish to the top of the rounded fireguard (it was winter by now and we had a proper fire) we took precautions at once. He was obviously heading for the two inch gap above the guard, so we got a piece of wire netting, wired it firmly to the top of the guard, left sufficient at either side to bend round the fireplace hood when the guard was in place – and with that at the top and a pair of heavy brass firedogs wedged against the bottom, we reckoned we'd pretty well taken care of that little hazard. We had, too, though I don't know which surprised people more. Coming in and seeing the fireplace wired up like No-Man's Land for no apparent reason, or coming in when Seeley was clinging to the top of it and one could see them thinking, 'Good God! They've got *another* of them!'

Not only was the guard now pretty depressing-looking but it kept back some of the heat, of course, so when we were going to be permanently in the room we took it away. Thus it was that Charles lit the fire as usual one morning and then we sat down at the other end of the room to have breakfast and Charles was just saying, with his cup halfway to his lips, that he thought, this morning, he'd get on with winter-washing the apple trees, when he suddenly yelled, slammed down the cup so hard it splashed coffee all over the tablecloth, and shot sideways up the room as if jerked by a string. I was sitting with my back to the fireplace and for the moment I was quite bewildered. Only when I turned round and saw him flat on his stomach on the hearthrug clutching a kitten as unrepentantly black as pitch did I realise what had happened.

The fire, said Charles, hadn't been drawing well. He'd just looked across and decided he'd have to re-light it after breakfast and at that moment a spark flickered up from the apparently dead coal, hovered for a moment in the draught, and then soared like a star up the chimney. As it did, Seeley, who'd been sitting on the hearthrug with the wistful waiting-for-Santa expression on his face which is why Siamese kittens get themselves on Christmas cards so often, soared after it and Charles, thanks to the fact that he'd been looking and also to the speed at which he'd moved, had been just in time to grab him before he vanished.

After that we had to keep a guard over the fireplace at all times and, as the old guard looked so dismal with the chicken wire tied to it, we decided to get a new one that fitted the fireplace properly. Wrought iron while we were at it, we thought, as we'd have to keep it there in the summer as well. As our fireplace is unusually wide to allow for log-burning we had to have the fireguard specially made, of course, and a pretty penny *that* little Siamese foible cost us.

Seeley also differed from Solomon over the ever-pressing question of where he had his earthbox. Solomon and Sheba had been born in the cottage. On our bed, as a matter of fact; otherwise, their mother had insisted, she wouldn't have kittens at all. Thanks to her equally determined insistence that they had to be brought up upstairs, because only there were they safe from the kidnappers she imagined were lying in wait for them round every corner, they'd spent the first impressionable weeks of their lives in the spare room and there, as a matter of course, they'd had their earthboxes. As far as Solomon was concerned it was more than a matter of course; it was a law of the Medes and Persians. His box had always been there; he expected it to be there; if it was anywhere else his stomach wouldn't work and the entire village was told about it *molto voce.*

After fourteen and a half years of following in Solomon's footsteps Sheba also took it for granted her box would be there. Not for regular use, of course. There were super places among the dahlias for general digging. But for when we were out, or if it was raining, or at night when there were foxes around the cottage.

Not so Seeley. He'd been brought up in a place where there weren't any foxes or traffic and so they were able to have a cat-door. He couldn't understand for the life of him why we didn't have one – but he knew jolly well where it ought to be, and when he wanted to attend to the wants of Nature (which, since he drank so much, was about ten times as often as a normal kitten) he made for the kitchen door and shouted at it. During the day we could let him out into the garden, whither he scurried with great intent and usually dug a good six holes before he was satisfied that one was properly propitious. But at night we put him in the hall and indicated the way upstairs.

Seeley just couldn't get used to the idea at all. He hoped he wouldn't be blamed for being Dirty, he would complain, his blue eyes round with concern as he seated himself in the corner by the window on his plastic washing-up bowl. Even when he found he wasn't blamed, he still didn't like going upstairs in the dark. He was, after all, only a baby. He hadn't been born in the place like Solomon and Sheba. And venturing in complete darkness through a strange hall, up the strange stairs and into a place that he knew his mother certainly wouldn't have approved of his using, was a very worrying matter for a little cat.

So it was that we had to put the lights on for him and make encouraging remarks from the bottom of the stairs while he climbed them very reluctantly, not liking to leave us behind. So it was that, discovering a plastic bowl that looked exactly like his spare-room earthbox only in a far more sensible place (outside the sitting-room door, en route to the kitchen, and therefore in the direction that cat-doors and earthboxes were intended to be) he promptly started to use it. And thus it was that, having for years used a plastic bowl in which to keep small coal for backing up the fire (as being lighter than a hod and not so likely to damage the fireplace canopy when I swing it at it and inevitably hit it) we now began to find it suspiciously damp. Sometimes, if there wasn't any coal in it, it was, quite frankly, awash. It happened so mysteriously, too – but it was no good blaming it on the fairies. Leading from the bowl was always a trail of little black footprints.

Then came the night when we had visitors and Seeley (in this he was exactly like Solomon) was keeping very quiet in case any of them were planning to Kidnap him. He sat around behind chairs; he lurked; he looked owlish. When anyone spoke to him he didn't answer; just his eyes grew rounder than ever. I put him out in the hall once in case he wanted his box, but a little white shadow slipped swiftly back round the door again and vanished under the table. It never occurred to me that, with strangers there, he'd be even more reluctant to go upstairs by himself. It never occurred to me either that he couldn't possibly – being Seeley – have gone for five solid hours without paying a visit to his box. Eventually the visitors went, however, lingering at their car doors to comment on the freshness of the Valley air at night; on the mysterious sound of the stream gushing past in the darkness; on the ceiling of stars that shone like diamonds over the pines... Charles, seeing them off, agreed equably with every word. He didn't look so unruffled when he came back indoors, however. He only hoped nobody had *noticed*, he said worriedly. And when I asked 'Noticed what?' he said 'Seeley using the coal-scuttle.'

Seeley, it seemed, hadn't been able to hold out. And, not wishing to disturb Polite Company (or, which was far more likely, not wanting to go upstairs on his own) he'd done the only thing he could think of... an extension, in his infant mind, of using the plastic bowl... and used the copper coal-scuttle in the sitting-room. Charles had spotted him sitting in it with a look of unmistakeable earnestness on his face. Who else had seen him, goodness only knew. All we did know was that, while Solomon himself had never used the coal-scuttle, in principle this was, exactly, Solomon.

Seeley was, in fact, far more like Solomon than he was unlike him, and was following increasingly in his footsteps every day. In the way he looked, the way he reasoned, in his bumble-footedness – and, very markedly, in his ever-increasing desire to be an adventurer.

I had quailed at the thought of that prospect from the beginning. All those acres of woods and moorlands and invitingly grassy lanes, and Seeley so very small, unaware of the dangers... Sometimes I wonder if that is why Siamese kittens are so white. So that when they set out on these inevitable treks of theirs, their mothers can spot them easily and fetch them back. The smudge on the nose that later spreads into the handsome Siamese mask; the little black socks that eventually become the elegant Siamese stockings; the dusky tipped ears and the absurd little black matchstick tail that will one day be a slender, curving whip – these they presumably carry to prove that they *are* Siamese, in case they meet up with another member of the clan. Nature provides no real camouflage for the young Siamese, however, who is unmistakeably, outstandingly, white – which only goes to show how well Nature knows what she is doing.

After his coming there was a week or so of deceptively peaceful days when, if I let him out, I had only to glance out of the door and there he was, gravely surveying the world from the wall adjoining the kitchen, or peering wide-eyed round the corner at the lawn – and then Seeley, like Solomon before him, was away.

On to the hillside behind the cottage to begin with, where he stood out white as a button mushroom against the turf. A very tentative little mushroom, especially when he was stalking Annabel and then she'd snort, turn round to look at him – and suddenly, to his consternation, the tables were reversed.

He was fascinated by Annabel. Had been ever since he
first looked out of the kitchen window and there she was,
up on the hillside, like a great big perambulating furry rug.
She was obviously the reason for his venturing on to the
hillside – though it was one thing to be trailing intrepidly
after a hairy monster and quite another to have the monster
looking at him. He would sit down then – Mum having
presumably told him always to look Nonchalant in time
of danger and never to run away. He would manage the
nonchalant part, too, looking unconcernedly up the
hillside, casually back over his shoulder and every now
and then glancing fleetingly up at Annabel who towered,
head lowered, above him. He would at the same time
be trembling like an aspen and patently thankful when I
rushed to snatch him to safety.

He persevered, though. When she came to the door for
titbits in the morning he would advance staunchly across
the kitchen to sniff at her nose. Then he discovered that
if he got on the table he could, very daringly, waylay her
ears. When they reached the stage where Annabel – or so it
seemed to us as onlookers – stood there with her ears stuck
forward deliberately waiting for Seeley to play with them,
his confidence knew no bounds.

'No, leave them!' I said the first time Seeley walked
between her legs as she stood in the yard and Charles, afraid
she might stamp on him, would have leapt to the rescue.
And Seeley ambled as trustingly as if he were going through
a set of croquet hoops and Annabel drooped her underlip
benevolently – a sign we knew of old when Annabel was
feeling motherly – and so we were encouraged to try
putting him on her back. He took to it as to the manner

born, crouched flat on her shaggy coat for a better grip and riding like that first for a few tentative steps across the yard, then through the gate into the lane, and eventually round the corner and up the steeply rising track to the field where she grazed behind the cottage.

Father Adams was rapt with admiration when he saw it. 'Regular little cough drop he's going to be,' he said as Seeley swayed past him clinging to Annabel with great concentration.

He was right there. A few days of that and our cough drop discovered that he could, after riding Annabel into her field, leap off her back, dash madly through her wire fence, and be up in the pine woods before anybody could stop him. There he would flit, deliberately tantalising us, among the trees. As he grew bolder he began to venture into the depths. Charles hadn't put up the cage yet – partly because he hadn't got round to it and, in any case, one could hardly pen a kitten on the lawn in winter. Better to let him exercise his legs and bring him in, was Charles's advice.

It exercised my legs, too. There I was, experiencing the old familiar feelings all over again. The apprehension when I saw him belting up the hillside towards the treeline. The chagrin when I chased him and he just beat me to it into the depths. The frustration when I followed him and he nipped, quite deliberately, into a bramble patch where he knew I couldn't follow. And the panic when I called him and there was nothing but silence.

There was also the heartfelt relief when, after ages of searching, calling and running madly up and down the lane to cover his possible exit points, there would be a plaintive little 'Waaah' from the interior, a scampering in the undergrowth, and – safe after all from the foxes and badgers and dogs we'd imagined in wait at every turn – a smudge-nosed little white figure danced light-heartedly into the lane ahead of us. 'Like Christmas with all the bells ringing' was how Charles described the feeling.

My mind was now several worries ahead, however. How long, now that he'd discovered the woods behind us, would it be before he started venturing into our own wood across the lane in front of us? And from there up into the orchard, where Charles kept those blasted bees?

EIGHT

When, two years previously, Charles said he was thinking of taking up bee-keeping, I said Oh No We Weren't. We had enough problems with Annabel and the cats, I said, without adding bees to the mixture.

It was for his fruit trees, Charles explained. They needed cross-pollination.

They certainly needed something. We have nearly a hundred trees in the orchard – apples and pears, and plums and damsons and cherries. In spring it is a picture that would inspire the most hardened artist, what with the blossom, the butterflies and Annabel knee-deep in emerald grass – but come the autumn we are always disappointed over the fruit. Due to the altitude, perhaps, or to the fact that the soil isn't really suited to fruit growing, or that Charles encourages the birds and if they don't eat the blossom they eat the fruit... 'Lack of pollination,' said Charles on this occasion, showing me the bit in his fruit book where it said that bees could make a difference of as much as forty per cent in the size of a crop.

I couldn't counter that, of course. And there is the fact that Charles likes honey and eats a pound to himself a week. So eventually I agreed to our having them. So long as they were kept right at the top of the orchard, I said, where they couldn't sting me or the animals. And so long as I, personally, wasn't expected to have anything to do with them.

Famous last words again, of course. The bees arrived one muddy day in February. The man from whom Charles had bought them — who assured him that he was giving up bee-keeping because he was going to live in town and not from any ulterior motive – came over to help with their installation. But the orchard is on a steeply sloping hillside, and a beehive with bees in it is very heavy – and, said their former owner, he'd nailed a piece of wood across their doorway to keep them in, but it would be just as well not to drop the hive, in case the roof came off... That was logical enough. So guess who had to tag along with the other two, supporting their ankles as they climbed so they wouldn't slip, going up through the mud? Right in the position where, if they *had* slipped, twenty thousand bees would have landed on me like water tipped out of a bucket?

We got them installed without mishap, however, and next day Charles, immensely brave inside the rather derelict bee-veil he'd acquired along with the bees, took the wood off the doorway and waited for his bees to come out.

It was some days before they did. There has to be warmth in the sun before the bees start making their first flight after the winter, but eventually Charles came back to report that there were one or two out... and the next day one or two more... and a few days later that calamity had struck. There were a lot of dead bees outside the hive.

Things weren't as bad as they looked, however. From reference to the bee book it seemed that it wasn't due to any of the bee diseases but that they'd probably run out of food. It was necessary to give them supplies at once – though not, I imagine, at quite the speed that Charles insisted on, where, surrounded by unwashed breakfast dishes, I hastily made bee-candy while he stood by ready to rush it up to them the minute it cooled.

It cooled pretty fast, too. By the time I'd managed to pour three lots into saucers, the rest had set solid in the saucepan and it took me days to get it out.

Have you ever tasted bee candy? It looks exactly like white fudge. We liked it. Annabel liked it so much that, having been given some of the scrapings, she spent the rest of the morning lurking on the slope behind the kitchen window, licking her lips and looking in to see if we were making some more. Most important of all, the bees liked it. Charles put it, a cake at a time, in the top of the hive. It took them a week to get through the first cake. After that they ate it at such a rate that every couple of days, it seemed, I was making bee candy and chipping away at the saucepans.

Eventually I was able to change to bee syrup, however, which is far easier than making candy. Candy is for winter feeding – when the bees rarely come out at all and if you give them food with too much water content they foul the hive and die.

They were coming out now, though. First in their dozens, then in their hundreds, and finally, as the weather grew warmer and warmer, in their thousands. It was at this stage that Charles, who by this time had worn a well-defined path up the hillside to watch them, noticed a long black tail proceeding airily up it one morning. Solomon, going to See What Was Up At The Top. Fortunately it was a dull day for a change and the bees were staying indoors, because when Charles caught up with him, Solomon was rubbing his head against a corner of the beehive and purring. There wasn't a bee in sight – but, said Charles, they were purring pretty loudly themselves, inside the hive. That was the next thing – rushing up the track after Solomon who, having never gone near that end of the orchard before, which was why we'd put the bees up there, now acted as if he were an electric tram, and up the trail to the hive was the only possible way he *could* go. Eventually he abandoned this in favour of a mouse hole by Annabel's stable, however, and as Solomon had a one-track mind and we knew that mousewatching would now be the order of the day for weeks, we were able to relax a little.

All this time the bees were taking in the pollen, which they use in rearing their young. They carried willow pollen and hazel pollen and hawthorn pollen... I had to take Charles's word for how marvellous it was to see them staggering manfully up the landing board with a fat little yellow bag on each hind leg. I still wouldn't go near the hive myself. When at last I did see them working at close quarters it was because the hawthorn was over, the elderflower wasn't out yet, and to fill in time they started coming into the garden, on the Oriental poppies.

They had a marvellous time on those. Instead of buzzing from floret to floret, as they had to do with the hawthorn, the bees would get on to a poppy, scuff furiously on the stamens like a puppy scuffing on a doormat... this filled the bags on their back legs like an automatic hopper and in no time at all the bee was off again. Burgundy all over where it had been burrowing in the stamens, and with two little bags of burgundy pollen slung beneath it like bombs beneath a plane.

It was fascinating to watch. I might even have become a beekeeper myself if at that point Charles hadn't got himself stung. Not when he was up at the hive, either, when in any case he'd have had his veil on, but while he was standing at quite a distance, interestedly watching them work. A guard bee apparently got suspicious of him and came down to warn him off. Then it got tangled in his hair, stung him on the head when it couldn't get out again – and the first I knew was his charging down through the orchard yelling for me to help him. That was sooner said than done. The bee was still buzzing madly in his hair. *I* didn't want to touch it. So I did the only thing I could think of and banged him on the head.

It despatched the bee all right. According to Charles it nearly despatched him as well. I hit him so hard I drove the sting right into his head, he said. The bee was on the front of his head when I hit it and the sting, when I found it, was at the back, but he always insisted I'd banged it in.

Anyway, I removed the sting, he had a bit of a swelling on his head but it wasn't much... There was nothing *to* it when you got used to it, he assured me, with the confidence of somebody who, after trembling for days, has just plucked up courage to be vaccinated.

He didn't say that the next time he was stung. This was some weeks later, during which time he'd acquired a better bee-veil, never went into the orchard without it, and had become quite adept at putting on supers. These are the boxes, containing frames, which one puts on a hive for the bees to fill with honey. You take off the roof, give the bees a puff of smoke to keep them quiet, bung on the super and Bob's your Uncle.

Unfortunately the time comes when you have to take the supers off again and this isn't nearly so easy. The bees have a habit of fastening everything down with a kind of glue they make called propolis, and unless one remembers to put vaseline on the edges of the supers first – which Charles didn't – you have to prise them apart with a thing like a crowbar. Charles, too, was proposing to take off several supers. He'd gone up the previous night and found the landing-board of the hive inches deep in bees. When he looked inside the roof he found them inches deep in there, too. He thought they were getting ready to swarm, which was something he wanted to avoid. So he rang a bee-keeping friend who advised him to put in another half brood box. That would keep them quiet, said his friend. They wouldn't swarm with extra room to breed in.

The snag to that was that the brood box is at the very bottom of the beehive, under the supers, which meant taking all the supers off first. Anyway, up went Charles next morning with his smoke-gun, his bee-veil and the newly-prepared brood box, and I was in the garden getting new potatoes for lunch, and everything was beautifully quiet and peaceful until I suddenly heard Charles once more running and shouting for help.

It wasn't just one bee this time. They were after him, when he shot out of the orchard, like a particularly violent eruption of Vesuvius. I rushed to the kitchen, got a bucket of water, dashed valiantly back to throw it over him – only to be deterred by the realisation that a bucket of water wasn't going to make much impression on that lot, and then they'd be after me… Charles was yelling in anguish 'Light some cardboard!' (Cardboard being the stuff one burns m the smoke-gun, but where to find any, and how to light it quickly when I got it, I just couldn't think.)

What I did was to crumple some newspapers, pile them on the lawn against the wall, light them and call to Charles to run down the lane and hang *over* the wall. He did, and the wall protected him from the flames, and the smoke drove off the angry bees… We weren't out of the wood even yet, though.

I got him into the kitchen and extracted the stings. Ten on one wrist where his glove had slipped when the smoke-gun failed, four on the other wrist and one on each of his knees, where he'd gone up in his oldest gardening trousers with holes in them. And while he was saying he felt queer but he really must go back, he'd left the hive in pieces all over the ground, there was a tap at the front door and there, when I answered it, was one of our neighbours, particularly renowned for her politeness, saying she was awfully sorry to trouble us, but one of our bees had stung her.

On her head, she said. As she was coming round the corner. Please would I mind getting it out?

She has thick hair. I couldn't find the blasted thing. I rushed indoors again, grabbed a towel from the bathroom, rushed back out, rubbed her head madly till the bee fell

out, got out the sting and bunged on the mixture of bicarb.
and water I'd been putting on Charles…

Sorry I couldn't stop, I said, but we were in a bit of a flap
at the moment. So she went off, and Charles came round
the corner saying he Must get back to his Bees, and then
– honestly it was just like something out of Greek tragedy
– he suddenly sagged at the knees and collapsed clean out
on the doorstep.

It was the concentrated effect of the bee-stings, of course.
It affects some people more than others. I hadn't been stung
myself but I was pretty well in a coma, too, by that time. I
helped him up – for some reason having it in my mind that
I must get him round to the kitchen, though why I can't
imagine… and there we were staggering round the outside
of the cottage like a pair of wounded comrades… A fat lot
of good it did when we got to the kitchen, too, because
Charles immediately said 'Uuuuh' and fainted again, right
by the side of the refrigerator.

I got him into an armchair in the living-room with
his feet up and gave him some whisky. It wasn't, I knew,
very good for his ulcer, but I remembered reading once
that they give cowboys whisky for rattlesnake bite, and
somewhere I'd also read that bee-stings are akin to snake
venom. Charles's ulcer won, however, and he immediately
announced that he felt sick. So I dumped a bucket beside
him, moved Annabel from where she was grazing in
the lane, checked that the car windows were up because
the cats were sleeping in it and by this time the garden
was full of bad-tempered bees, and fled to do Charles's
other behest, which was to find somebody to put the hive
together again.

I made three attempts before I found someone. Charles's friend was out. Another bee-keeper I rang didn't have a car – at least, he said he didn't. The man who eventually came turned out to be the chairman of the local bee-keeping association, and from the twitch on his lips when he saw Charles laid out in the chair with the bucket at his side and heard the; story of his misadventures we were obviously going to be the subject, in the not too distant future, of a pretty effective lecture on How Not To Be A Beekeeper.

Even more so, I reckoned, when he came back and announced that the bees hadn't been going to swarm, there were no signs at all of any queen cells and *how*, he enquired (having picked it up on his way back from the beehive and realised that that was the cause of the trouble) did Charles light his smoke-gun?

From the bottom up, Charles informed him frailly. And of course it should have been from the top down, only Charles had acquired the smoke-gun along with the bees and there weren't any instructions with it.

'Better luck next time!' said the expert as he went. Charles, when he'd gone, said there wasn't going to be a next time. The bees would have to go.

Bees definitely get a grip on one, however. By four o'clock, when Charles had recovered sufficiently to have a cup of tea, he'd decided to keep the bees to pollinate the fruit trees but not to go near them himself. By six o'clock – well, he might occasionally go up and watch them, but he wouldn't go near the hive. By seven o'clock he was going to take up bee-keeping properly again, but first he'd see his doctor, to make sure he wasn't allergic.

He didn't, of course. By next day he was saying he'd never felt better in his life, the stings must have done him good. Which was why, the following day, there was such consternation when he got stung again.

A bee must have crawled up under his shirt while he was in the orchard watching them, got onto the waistband of his trousers, and then – a good ten minutes after he'd come safely down from the hive and was about to have a cup of tea – it fell down inside his trousers and stung him indignantly on the stomach.

He didn't mention about bee stings being good for him then. 'They've got me again!' he was shouting as he came charging out of the kitchen. 'Quick they've got me worse than ever!' They hadn't, actually. It was only one bee-sting. It was just that it was in a tender spot. But with Charles leaping about and howling, and my being panic-stricken in case he *was* allergic and this sting might finish him off – sometimes I felt really beleaguered.

NINE

He survived all right, but there was still the honey to be extracted before we could consider the season safely over, and from what I could gather that was the trickiest job of the lot.

The procedure is that one goes out one night at dusk, removes the roof of the hive, lifts off (with a cloth over the top to stop the bees coming out) the super or supers from which one intends to take the honey and inserts, above the rest of the hive, a flat wooden cover with an escape hatch in it. One then replaces the supers and the roof and tiptoes away, the idea being that throughout the night the bees at work in the supers will make their way down through the escape hatch to the brood chamber. They cannot, theoretically, get back again, because it is a one-way-only escape hatch, and the following day one should, provided the bees have co-operated properly, be able to lift off the supers (empty now of bees and brimming, one hopes, with honey), carry them back to the house and extract the honey at leisure.

One snag we had been warned of by friends was to make sure we did the extracting in an absolutely bee-proof room. And clear away every trace of the operation afterwards, they said, or the bees would be after us like hornets. They'd once done the extracting in their kitchen. They'd closed all the doors and windows, and those of the conservatory beyond the kitchen, and thought they were doubly safe. There was a small hole in a pane of the conservatory glass, however. Only about an inch across, high up in a corner, but the bees had tracked it down like Apaches on the warpath. When they looked up from their extracting, said our friends, it was like being in an aquarium. There were thousands of bees in the conservatory, literally swimming past the kitchen window in shoals, looking angrily in at them and searching for a hole in that.

They coped all right, of course. They were practised bee-keepers. A sting or two meant nothing to them and their bees were quiet bees. Not at that immediate moment, perhaps, but it only needed a few puffs of smoke and the empty frames put out into the garden to placate them (the bees clean out every drip of honey then and take it back to the hive) and everything was back to normal.

With us, not only were we non-experienced bee-keepers (I, in fact, was still very firmly not a bee-keeper at all); but Charles was suspect of being allergic and we had the worst-tempered bees it was possible to have. This wasn't just my opinion, either. Bees, it seems, differ in temperament according to their origin as surely as does the human race.

Austrian and Caucasian bees, for instance, are as docile as it is possible for a bee to be; the Black, or English type, is a stolid worker and will go out on the dullest summer's day... their docility couldn't always be relied upon, said the reference book, but they had none of the wickedness of the Cyprian or Syrian varieties. At the debit end of the scale *are* the Cyprian and Syrian – and ours, it was obvious from the book (and wouldn't you have bet on it?) were the Syrians. Striped black and yellow; working like mad when the sun came out but not, apparently, so keen to work on sunless days as the phlegmatic English Black (what scope, it occurred to us, for a student of environment and heredity!) and, unfortunately, very hasty-tempered, and difficult to handle.

The village, meanwhile, was watching our activities with interest. Miss Wellington telling us how she was looking forward to sampling some of our honey. Father Adams asking regularly how thic old stingers was gettin' on then – and proceeding, before we could tell him, to acquaint us with the latest hair-raising story about bee-keeping that he remembered, had read about in the newspapers or (we sometimes suspected) invented.

When he read about somebody who'd been chased by a swarm, for instance, and had to take refuge in a telephone kiosk, he stumped down immediately to tell us. 'Aint got no kiosks round these parts,' he said to Charles. 'Reckon thees'd have to keep on runnin'.' Then he heard of a horse that had been stung on the rump and it bolted. 'Thees't want to watch out,' he said portentously to me. At that time I was riding, two or three times a week, a horse called Rory whose owner didn't have time to exercise him. He was undisciplined. I hadn't ridden much for years. All I needed to give me confidence was the thought of Rory being spurred on by a bee...

Something had to be done about the honey, though, if only for the sake of our *amour propre* around the village. So one night in September, a week before we were due to go on holiday, Charles went up to insert the escape hatch in the hive. I waited in the lane with the garden spray at the ready. That, I'd read in the bee-book, was a help in deterring angry bees. Everything went all right on that occasion, however. Charles was quite exhilarated when he came back to report that they'd been buzzing all around him but he'd coped with them perfectly. Gave them a whiff or two of the old smoke, he said. No trouble at all putting the board in. He was really getting the hang of this bee-keeping business at last.

I wasn't so certain, which was why the next evening, a few minutes after he went up to bring down the supers, I sallied forth myself. I was wearing trousers, gum boots, one of Charles's old macintoshes tied round my waist with string (otherwise it was too loose and the bees could get up inside) and Charles's thick winter gloves. I also had on my riding hat, which happens to be the only hat with a peak I possess – and, on top of that, a veil. Not a bee-keeper's veil because, being determinedly not a bee-keeper, I didn't have one. This was something I'd devised some years before, when we'd gone camping in the Camargue. A collapsible muslin meat-cover with a crinoline of mosquito netting sewn round it. We'd hung one each over our beds in the tent and with the meat-cover forming a dome overhead and the netting tucked into our sleeping bags we'd slept peacefully, secure and unstung.

It looked a bit peculiar, nevertheless – and it looked even more peculiar worn over a riding hat. Needs must when the devil drives the barrel organ, however, as Charles so often says. *I* didn't want to get stung. I had a nasty feeling that if I wasn't out there Charles would get stung himself. And this was the only protection I could think of.

I also had it in mind to light a fire... in a bucket just inside the back gate this time, I thought... Charles might not make it, carrying the heavy supers, as far as the lower lawn... Which was why the occupants of a car going slowly up the lane a little later (a courting couple by the look of it, hunting for a place to park), happened with obvious astonishment on the edifying spectacle of me, wearing a riding hat with a meat-cover and mosquito net on top, crouched in the dusk over a bucket with holes in it, feeding a fire with damp hay and raising cloud upon cloud of smoke.

If they'd glanced up to the right of them (only they didn't, they were too busy looking at me), they'd have seen another edifying sight. Charles coming down the opposite hillside, also wearing an old mackintosh tied round the waist with string, on *his* head a big, box-framed veil that made him look like a man from Mars, and carrying a large square box wrapped carefully in a bath-towel. Another of my ideas, the bath-towel – to keep in any bees that hadn't gone through the hatch. And, by George, it was a useful one. Under its covering of bath-towel the super was humming like Battersea Power Station.

There were only about a dozen in there, said Charles. There must have been a little hole somewhere and they'd managed to get back again. He'd only brought down one of the supers, though – he thought he'd leave the second one till tomorrow.

It was just as well he did. According to the instruction book one now removed the frames from the super (ten of them, hanging like photographic plates from a rack); gently brushed off any bees which remained on them; took off, with a knife dipped in hot water, the layer of beeswax which covered the comb; put the frames four at a time in a cylindrical extractor which looks like an ice cream churn; turned the handle steadily, and out flowed the honey like manna.

Gently brush off the bees, my foot. Charles's dozen turned out to be about fifty. Creeping out of crevices, crawling menacingly over the frames, some still working with their heads stuck down in the combs. Try to brush that lot off gently and they came at us like a nest of scorpions... So there we were when the courting car came past again (either having failed to find a parking place or a bit apprehensive, perhaps, after what they thought they'd seen on the journey up), and this time they really had their money's worth.

There were two of us there now, still in our arresting headgear, and the damp hay had dried out and was blazing up merrily like a Guy Fawkes bonfire. What Charles and I were actually doing, waving our arms above the flames and leaping like a couple of Dervishes, was passing the frames through the smoke to dislodge the bees and then jumping and ducking instinctively because, protected though we were, bees coming into the attack like rifle bullets are a bit unnerving in the dark. What they thought we were doing was another matter, but I bet their guesses didn't include bee-keeping.

We got rid of the bees at last, however, took the frames down to the kitchen and extracted the honey. Having said quite a lot about bees already I will forbear to describe that operation other than to say that we got honey all over the place (we had been warned that we would) and that it took us from nine at night until one o'clock next morning... this included washing the doors, floor, walls and ourselves, of course, as well as actually extracting the honey... and that when we finished we had exactly twelve jars of the confounded stuff.

Charles said the bees must have been eating the honey and we really ought to have extracted it in August. He also said he thought he'd leave the second super – a full twenty-eight pounds there must be in that one until we came back, refreshed, from Provence.

Marvellous it was, knowing we weren't going to have a repeat of that little performance before we went on holiday. Even more marvellous when, while we were actually *on* holiday, lying on a white-sanded beach beneath the pine trees, with the cicadas clicking happily behind us in the undergrowth and not a single bee in sight, Charles said he'd been thinking. If the bees felt that strongly about it, he said, he was going to let them keep that second super. It would save him feeding them, anyway, during the winter.

I felt as if I'd been reprieved. I swear even the hot Provençal sun shone suddenly brighter. A good five months before I need even *think* of bees – and maybe before the spring they'd have left home or died or something.

They didn't. On all that honey they grew even stronger. Bees, they say, start breeding in January if the weather is propitious and ours were so hard at it that by February we were having to feed them again.

In March one repaid Charles by stinging him. Far from his resistance having built up, as he kept telling me it was bound to have done, he had in fact become sensitised to bee-stings and this fresh sting just added to his content of bee-venom. In no time his face was like a pumpkin and when he woke me around three o'clock next morning to say he felt peculiar, all I could say was that he looked it. His eyes were sinister slits, his cheeks were huge rubber pouches, and his face and ears and neck were a blazing, fiery red.

That was an anxious night if ever there was one. I gave him aspirin, hoped for the best with his ulcer and waited with trepidation for the dawn. I also indulged in a soliloquy about Bees and Why We Had To Have Them and next morning Charles, with no more ado, was at the doctor's.

'*Do* you have to go on keeping them?' echoed the doctor and when Charles said Yes he did the doctor (obviously he'd met them like this before) sighed and wrote out a prescription. For tablets which Charles had to take for three weeks and they would then give him several months' immunity.

He was a bit more cautious after this, nevertheless, not being anxious to put his immunity to the test – which was why he put off making an inspection of the hive and in June the bees duly swarmed.

Bees, who work strictly to rule, swarm only in the afternoon, so this must have started on the day when, with some friends who were calling on us on their way to Cornwall, we went over to see the lions at Longleat. It was a still, sunny, swelteringly hot day – just right for watching lions on a make-believe *veldt*. Little did we know, however, as we watched them sunbathing on their platforms, lying posed majestically in prides and once, to our delight, came across a huge black-maned male lying lazily on his side beneath a bush, not three feet away from our car, of the stirring events that were going on in our own private nature reserve at home in the Valley.

When bees swarm they pitch, with the migrating queen, on a nearby tree or similar object while the scouts go out to look for another home. Sometimes they find one quickly and the swarm is away within an hour. Sometimes they are rather more fussy and the swarm stays on its tree overnight. This must have happened with us. It was around ten o'clock next morning when, still thinking of the lions, I went out into the garden – and I was never more surprised in my life than when I heard a noise like a giant humming top coming from over the hedge across the lane. I looked across to see what appeared to be a curtain of insects hovering in the air behind it – like gnats, only fifty times as frenzied; and then, even as I stared, unable to believe my eyes, the curtain was wafting away up the Valley like a water-spout, leaving behind it an abrupt, very noticeable silence.

Charles was aghast when I told him his bees had swarmed and we spent the rest of the day looking for them. He searched in the woods while I, keeping my fingers crossed and hoping we wouldn't find them, otherwise he'd have me up a tree or on somebody's roof as sure as eggs were eggs, did my share of patrolling in the Valley. It was so very quiet. No sound of cars or people. It is of days and scenery like this that people think of when they dream of old-time England. Up the lane, in the garden of a ruined cottage, a woodpecker sat on a post he was inspecting for insects. A big green woodpecker with a vivid scarlet crown, unmoving and silent, so I shouldn't see him as I passed. The stream splashed among the kingcups, a cuckoo called in the drowsy distance, there were bees and other insects drinking at the water's edge…

Bees drink in the ordered way they manage the rest of their existence. Always, according to the hive from which they come, from the same small stone or blade of grass. They sweep down, queue up on the landing stage, take in their quota of water and streak back, as if their lives depended on it, to the hive to which they belong. I watched them now with the eye of a Sherlock Holmes. Some, taking the water from a stone where the stream ran under our driveway, were zooming up, over the hedge and back to our own hive high in the orchard. Some, further up the Valley, were making for a different base… a fenced-in enclosure where another bee-keeper had some hives. Of our truant bees, ensconced by now somewhere deep in the forest, there was no sign at all. They'd be fetching water by now, of course – but from other springs out across the hills.

Eventually we gave up the search. I vastly relieved that we hadn't found them, Charles sadly bemoaning their loss. My sense of relief was slightly premature, however. A week later they swarmed again.

TEN

I didn't know it could happen. I really thought I was seeing things when I went out into the garden just after lunch and there they were at it again, whirling like inebriated Dervishes in exactly the selfsame spot.

This time they were coming in to settle, however, not taking off, as I'd seen them before. In a moment they were down and all was silence. You would never have known they were there. And what did I do *now*? I pondered perplexedly. Tell Charles and he'd go out and get stung? Or say nothing and, as we'd planned to do, go to town in peace?

Conscience wouldn't let me do that, so I told Charles, helped him on with his veil and gloves, made sure his smoke-gun was lighted properly and the garden spray was working and, with a feeling of direly impending doom, watched him set forth into battle.

The first sound that came over the hedge was a shout that he had found them. In an elder tree, he said; they couldn't have been more accessible. The second sound was that of the garden spray hissing steadily. Charles was busy quietening them. Unfortunately it seemed to annoy them instead, however, and the fountains of water I could see shooting high in the air were followed by an exclamation, and then clouds of agitated smoke.

Honestly, I said from my watching post down in the lane. First it was like a Firemen's Benefit and now he was sending up Indian smoke signals. What on earth had he got up there? A hive of Black Widow spiders?

They were stroppy, said Charles, his voice muffled by his veil... but he thought he had them in hand. So much so that a few minutes later he asked for a box and a handbrush with which to gather them up. The idea is that one sweeps the swarm into the box, up-ends it on the ground to form a temporary hive and leaves it like that until sundown. Then, when all the bees are in for the night, one rehouses the swarm in a new hive, along with the queen, and presto the job is done.

That, at least, is how most people do it. Charles kept asking for another box... and then another one... and then another one... while I pitched them frenziedly over the hedge. It took him five large boxes to gather up his erring swarm. They kept rising up at him, he said.

At last the job was finished, however. Charles, unstung, was back in the cottage, triumphantly singing. Five boxes of bees were reposing in the orchard, waiting for the evening, when Charles would go up to re-hive them. How *would* they manage in five boxes, I asked, when the queen could be only in one? Charles said he hoped they would eventually find their way into her box. It would make things so much easier in the evening.

So, greatly relieved, with a feeling of Raiders Past, I went light-heartedly up to the farm to get some eggs en route for town. Some for Charles's mother, some for my Aunt Louisa, leaving Charles to get changed and follow me up in the car.

I was quite a time at the farm, telling them about the swarm and how Charles had so cleverly captured it. I was rather surprised when I came out again and he wasn't waiting at the gate. Not unduly so, however. Charles is pretty good at achieving hold-ups.

When I got back to the cottage, though, and there was the car still in the drive and no sign of him whatsoever, only a peculiarly brooding silence over the place, I began to feel tottery at the knees. He'd been to look at those bees and got stung, I thought, and now he was lying stretched out starkly in the cottage... He wasn't inside the cottage so I next imagined him stretched out starkly in the car, He wasn't (I could scarcely bring myself to look in it) there, so he must be lying stretched out over the hedge...

I was just, my world in pieces around me, about to go in and get the mosquito net and see if I could possibly drag him out (buried beneath crawling bees, I imagined him, and they'd undoubtedly get me as well and they wouldn't find either of us for days) when I heard footsteps coming down the Valley. It was Charles. Unstung, but mad as a hatter.

'What have you been *doing*?' I called with relief. 'They got away,' he shouted back. 'They can't have done,' I said. But they had.

He'd just been opening the gates, said Charles, when he'd heard this sudden buzzing across the lane. He'd looked across, there they were all in the air, and before he could do anything they were away. They'd swooped low across the garden (Charles's later interpretation was that they'd come down to say goodbye to him but at the time he'd leapt hastily into the car out of their reach); away up the Valley (by now Charles was out of the car and running after them); through the roof of the ruined cottage (he'd thought they were going to settle there, said Charles, but the darned things did a loop round the rafters and then zoomed out again); and away up over the hillside and into the forest.

We never found that lot either, but next day Charles got the bee-expert over and he went down through the hive. There were three more queens just ready to hatch, he reported; we'd have lost another two swarms if we hadn't called him in. Bees do this, it seems, if the hive is exceptionally prolific. Not just one swarm takes off, but up to four, till the hive is reduced in size. As to why that swarm had got away from Charles... the first swarm, said the expert, had had the old queen at its head. When *she* came down she'd wait till the scouts came to lead her to her new home... in our case she'd waited till next morning... and if we'd captured her, she would have stayed and so would the rest of the swarm. The subsequent swarms, however, are led by virgin queens. Just hatched, said the expert, and flighty and restless, like young maids the whole world over. He'd never known a virgin swarm that did stay put unless you locked 'em in to hold the queen.

So there we were. We were certainly learning about bees. There was more to it than he'd thought, said Charles, considerably chastened. She was still looking forward to tasting our honey, cooed Miss Wellington whenever we saw her.

She didn't get any. We didn't take even twelve pounds of it that season. The swarms had carried off most of it when they absconded and the bees still in the hive would need the rest, to feed them through the coming winter.

It was the bees still in the hive I was worried about in connection with Seeley. Next year, when they'd built up again and were ready to sting people, it would be a new little cat who was venturing forth. Solomon and Sheba had been grown cats when we had the bees and they'd met up before with individual ones. How could a little kitten know about a hive?

We'd do something about them before the spring, Charles assured me. Put wire netting around them... maybe let someone else have them... they took up a lot more time than he'd thought they would. Come the spring, I thought resignedly, I bet he'd get bee fever all over again, and I'd be making bee candy and haring to everybody's rescue...

There were months yet to spring, however, and I had more immediate things to worry about. Like the question of keeping up with Seeley's appetite, and his vanishing into the woods, and the growing signs of depredation around the place.

'Hope springs eternal in the human breast' is undoubtedly the motto of every Siamese cat owner. The cats rip the chair-covers, turn carpets into remarkable imitations of astrakhan, smash china till you'd think they had shares in a pottery… and still, when the owner replaces the article, he imagines that this time all will be well. With one or two precautions, perhaps, like putting rugs over vulnerable furniture, moving china from the route of Siamese steeplechases and, when one catches the culprits at it, ordering them firmly, very sternly, to desist…

It never works, of course. Some friends of ours took precautions, when they were having some armchairs recovered, to the extent of consulting with the buyer of a large furniture store as to the most suitable Siamese-proof material he could suggest. Now *that*, he said, being an enthusiast in his profession, would make a really interesting experiment, and one that might help lots of other suffering cat-owners… So he provided them with samples of materials which they left around tacked casually onto boards… large boards, said our friends, to simulate the backs of chairs…

It was obvious the burnt-orange boucle wasn't the answer; that finished up like sacking with holes in it (the same colour, too) within days. It was obvious the charcoal tweed wouldn't do, either; the colour was all right but it now had a fur-fabric nap. Finally they settled on a dusky green, tight-woven… I suppose you'd call it a linen rep. The cats hadn't so much as looked at that one, said their owners; the buyer said it obviously didn't titillate their claws.

They hadn't looked at it because why the heck should they, surrounded by boucle and tweed and strong-claw-making moquette? Once the experimental panels had been taken away, though, and in their place stood three chairs resplendent in tight-drawn green linen... it titillated their claws then all right, said their owners; they'd had the backs out of those chairs within *weeks*. No, it *hadn't* been of use to provide them with stropping boards. The green chairs were their Mecca and nothing else.

We'd gone through it all ourselves, of course. Goodness knows how many hearthrugs Solomon had ruined, stropping exuberantly in the middle (to test his Strength, he said). We'd tried putting a car-rug down when we were out of the room but that hadn't been any good. Solomon merely played tunnels under the car rug and – now we couldn't see him, he said excitedly, so we didn't know who was doing it, did we? – stropped harder on the hearthrug middle than ever.

There was the hide armchair in the hall, reduced by Sheba to a striking example of shagreen with holes in it. There was Solomon's demolition of the staircarpet and Solomon's morning exercises round the bed... He'd pulled himself up and down the bed-base so heartily for years that the stuffing now stuck out in tufts. It was no good trying to stop him if doing it, either. It made him feel good, he said.

Why, after all our experience, we should have I thought that Seeley was going to be different... but that was the hope springing eternal bit. He looked such a harmless little kitten, too. One couldn't imagine him doing any damage.

We soon learned. It must have been about his second day with us that, having shut him into the hall to try to have our lunch in peace, we decided to let him in because we couldn't stand his yelling any longer. It couldn't be good for him, either, said Charles, crying his little heart out like that... So he opened the door and I was still laughing at the way Seeley shot the length of the room like a greyhound straight from the trap, when he flashed back over my shoulder and landed smack in the middle of my plate. He'd been making for the armchair behind my dining-chair as a take-off board for the table. *He* hadn't been charging up the room at random.

Thereafter he made for that chair whenever he came into the room. Either as a quick way on to the table if we were sitting at it, as a ricochet spot or a smart bit of show-off if we weren't, or to drag himself round on his back when he was bored… all the more so when he discovered that it got me hopping mad.

It did make me mad, too. The ricochet bit was clever. Seeley dashing into the room, leaping in full flight to hit the back of the chair at a Wall of Death angle with all four feet as he passed and then galloping on as if in a circus ring was most spectacular indeed, and always earned a round of applause from his onlookers. But Seeley throwing himself on to his back, clawing his way noisily and deliberately round the bottom of a practically brand-new loose-cover and then pausing, still on his back and watching with one canny blue eye round the corner to see what I was going to do about it, made me very mad indeed. So I shouted at him, said he was a horrible little cat, which was just what he was waiting for and, with a look of fiendish glee on his face, he careered on round the bottom of the chair.

After that Seeley dragging himself along one side of the chair, waiting to be scolded and then zipping at twice the speed round the back and along the other side, was a regular feature of the cottage day. So was Seeley exercising himself round the bed-base – which showed, said Charles consolingly, just how much he was growing to be like Solomon.

Not to be left out of things, Sheba now started her own stropping sessions on the dining-chairs. It was nice to see her feeling so good, I said, but I did wish she would find somewhere else... It was no good, of course. She'd strop on a chair to attract Seeley's attention; he'd come across to hide beneath it and poke a paw excitedly up at her; she'd poke him back and he'd start climbing up to get at her... Bang, before my eyes, went my tomato-covered chairs.

Bang went something else, too. Seeley, shut out in the hall at meal times, started in on the draught excluder round the door. He must have decided that if he could winkle that out he could get in through the resultant crack, so after a few indignant protests he would sniffle, sit down, and proceed with the task of removing the draught excluder. Yellow foam rubber it was, and scattered in clawed-out bits over the red hall carpet it was not only quite impossible to miss seeing it, but it looked exactly like crumbled sponge cake.

'What on earth...' demanded Miss Wellington, arriving with a collection box one morning after breakfast and seeing what appeared to be pieces of cake scattered hysterically all over the carpet. Not wanting her to go off and tell people I'd been throwing cakes at Charles I explained the situation in detail. About shutting Seeley out or else he got in the plates, and if we did shut him out, then he set to on the draught excluder...

I got no sympathy from Miss Wellington. She'd disapproved strongly of our having Seeley – partly because she'd been so fond of Solomon and thought having a new kitten so soon meant we'd been hardhearted over him ourselves, and partly because she thought it would upset Sheba. She'd come in one day, however, and Sheba had been lying in front of the fire, with a car-rug banked round her as always in winter, to keep out the draught from the door.

'And how's our little girl?' enquired Miss Wellington, going forward to stroke her. Then she stopped. From where he lay, tucked into Sheba's side with the red tartan rug round the pair of them, a little black pansy face was regarding her. Not quite like Solomon's yet, for his mask was still but a smudge. But it was Solomon's eyes that looked up at her before he yawned, stretched, and put a fat little black paw more comfortably across Sheba's neck.

'The Dear, Dear Boy,' said Miss Wellington. After which you'd think that Seeley had been entirely her own idea.

Now she said 'The Dear, Dear Boy' in quite a different manner. As if we'd had him chained in a dungeon, not merely shut in the hall so we could eat in peace. And if the dear, dear boy *had* chewed the draught excluder, her tone implied, she only hoped, for the sake of our consciences, he hadn't swallowed any.

He hadn't. Or if he had, it didn't hurt him. And if Miss Wellington had had to put up with his yelling…

Not that we objected to his voice. We delighted to hear it. We could detect a definite note of Solomon in it, and the note was growing. His way of stumping along saying 'Mrrr-mrrr-mrrr' to himself was enchanting, too. It was just that sometimes his voice was so overpowering. When he was in the hall, for instance, and roaring his head off to come in. Or when he had the woods in prospect and was demanding, very raucously, to be let out. He sounded like Solomon then, all right – and very much like his own father.

'Wanna! Wanna! WANNA! WANNA!' he would sit and howl, with his eyes closed, at the kitchen door. He would get quite carried away with the drama of it, too, and was always obviously quite surprised at himself when I interrupted him with 'And what do you think *you're* doing?'

'Please???' he would plead then, beguilingly, in his tiniest seagull voice.

ELEVEN

That was all very well, but he was becoming more adventurous every day and when we let him out we never knew what he was going to get up to. Come to that, we never knew what he was going to get up to if we kept him in, either. That first venture onto the table, for instance, when, with a mighty leap from the back of the armchair, he'd landed in my plate – that had given him a taste for taking flying jumps at things followed by spectacular skids. The skids were no accident, either. From the inevitability with which they occurred it was obvious that they were quite deliberate. He skidded across the table, skidded across the counter tops in the kitchen, skidded exuberantly across the bathroom floor like a small boy on a slide. One day he skidded through the kitchen door and out into the yard so fast that, when he tried to turn the corner of the cottage and head for the lawn, he fell flat on his stomach on the paving stones. Didn't Matter, he said, picking himself up and galloping dustily on. He was getting to be an Expert at Falling Down.

He was also getting to be an expert at falling off things. Those prodigious leaps didn't always work. Sometimes they landed him on the kitchen counter when there were dishes on it, or the table in the sitting-room when there were papers on it, and, with a wild scrabble, off would plop Seeley plus whatever he happened to have got his paws on. He broke so many plates and saucers that, against the day when it might occur to him to try for the mantelpiece, I stuck down all the china on that with strips of sticking plaster.

Better to be safe than sorry, I thought. I had my grandmother's Staffordshire figures up there. I didn't want to move them but I didn't want them smashed... or the Italian china cats, or the glass swan from Venice that Louisa gave me, or the big Willow Pattern platter that was Charles's grandmother's. So I anchored the lot with sticking plaster – and wouldn't you have bet on it? Seeley never so much as looked at the mantelshelf. Presumably it didn't offer the right possibilities for skidding. But, with the inevitability that follows anything I do as surely as it rains if I clean the cottage windows, someone came to tea a few days later who happened to be interested in Staffordshire china.

'Ah! Will Watch!' she exclaimed, heading for the mantelpiece as soon as she entered and reaching for the yellow-trousered gentleman on the left. Presumably, to air her knowledge, she would then have said 'Ah! Rob Roy!' and reached for the dour-looking Highlander on the right – but she didn't get that far. There was a slight sound of tearing as the plaster lifted a bit, but – anchored fore and aft by five pieces of Elastoplast – Will Watch stayed exactly where he was.

Her eyes widened as she looked at what was holding him – and at the strips on the china cats and on the glass Venetian swan. She was nothing if not urbane, however. 'Ah! Benares vases!' she said to bridge the uncomfortable pause – having sighted the big brass ewers at either end of the mantelpiece.

They weren't held down by Elastoplast. They hadn't been properly cleaned, either. Rushed for time as usual, I'd polished the fronts and handles before she came, bunged them back on the shelf confident that they gleamed like gilt in front and that nobody could possibly see the backs…

She did. She lifted them down, turned them round to examine the pattern, and I could have sunk through the floor when their unpolished reverses came into view. It was all his fault, I informed Seeley when she'd gone. And Seeley sat there as usual, looking back at me innocently.

He always did look innocent. We kept his toys – his ping-pong balls and his catnip mouse and the fur spider with a bell on it of which he was especially fond – in a china mug on the table by the wall. A cider mug, two-handled and very old. Not stuck down, because it hadn't occurred to me that it was necessary, on an out-of-the-way table by the wall. He looked as innocent as a Botticelli angel when, in the course of fishing out his spider, he managed to land the mug with a crash in the middle of the coal-scuttle.

All those years and Solomon had never done that, I wailed – rushing, as I anticipated, to pick up the pieces. All those years and he'd never done *that*, either, commented Charles, as I retrieved the mug and, to my amazement, it was still in one piece; Solomon would infallibly have had the handles off. And Seeley sat peering over the table edge, the picture of wide-eyed wonder. Must have been Sheba, he said.

He looked innocent when we found him locked unaccountably in the woodshed, too. At least, it would have been unaccountable except that I happened to be in the yard and saw him disappearing behind the shed with a purposeful look to his rear view – and, knowing that his next move could well be round the corner and up on to the hillside, I nipped smartly after him to see where he was going. I was just in time to see him vanish through a hole in the back of the shed. A hole which, filled as the woodshed is with bottles, baskets and Charles's odd bits and pieces, we didn't even know was there.

Seeley did. And when, the next moment, the wails of an Imprisoned Siamese, Absolutely in Dire Distress, Send for the Vet At Once and Better get the Police As Well... When the old familiar call that we knew so well from Solomon rent the air and Charles came running as usual with a look of apprehension on his face... we *would* have been flummoxed, too, that we had to undo a padlock to get him out, except that I had seen him going in through the back.

There he was, when Charles unlocked the door. Posed, more angelically than ever, on a pile of old wood shavings. 'How on earth did you get in there?' demanded Charles, who hadn't yet heard the story. He didn't know. Somebody *pushed* him in. Must have been Sheba, Seeley assured him soulfully.

So he proceeded through the winter. Happily playing the game of Locked In The Woodshed By Sheba; exploring the mysteries of the countryside; entwining himself in our lives with every day that passed.

Secretly I dreaded the thought of Christmas that year. Aunt Ethel and Louisa and Charles's family there... everything as it always had been, except for a dusky-faced cat no longer with us. I thought of Solomon a lot on Christmas Day. It was better than I'd anticipated, however. Annabel was there on the frosty lawn, eating her biscuits and carrots. Sheba was with us on her tomato-coloured chair, her paws tucked under her like a little sitting hen, squawking complacently when people spoke to her. And if my eyes wandered sometimes around the chattering, lamplit room – to where a cat with big bat ears had once watched us from under the table... to where a cat with a worried expression had once peered from under a chair... to where a cat, when he'd decided the visitors were Safe, had once sat holding Christmas court majestically on the hearthrug... now, in the self-same places, frolicked a little fat white kitten. Hiding beneath the table. Peering from behind the chair. Venturing forth, when he was sure that all was well, to play with his tail before the fire. The wheel had turned full circle. Seeley was carrying the lamp.

He not only carried it; he singed his whiskers on it. The bathroom at the cottage is on the ground floor, built back into the hill. In damp weather it condenses badly and to combat this we keep an oil-lamp burning behind the bath. An old-fashioned Aladdin table lamp, which just fits into the narrow space against the wall. Turned low for safety, it gives very little light – but the heat is sufficient to warm the wall; it smells, not of oil, but of old-time country warmth; and such light as it does give affords a mellow, mysterious dimness. So, it seemed, thought Seeley – who, when he asked to be let through the sitting-room door these nights, could be found not seated worriedly on the coal-bowl, as had been his initial wont, but sitting quietly on the mosaic surround of the bath.

Thinking, he said when we asked him what he was doing. Charles said he supposed it was all right to leave him with the lamp? Of course it was, I said, Solomon and Sheba had never touched it. It was therefore my fault, indubitably, that Seeley returned one night without his whiskers. The lamp, not meditation, had been the attraction – until at length, unable to contain his curiosity any longer, he'd plucked up courage to look down into the lamp-chimney and zing, as fast as lightning, he'd lost his whiskers.

'Just like Solomon,' said Sheba when she saw him. It was too, except that Solomon's whiskers had been chewed off affectionately by his mother, not singed off over a lamp. 'Growing more like him every day,' said Charles with apprehension.

Growing he was indeed. When we first had him he could hide under the armchairs, dart around like a clockwork mouse beneath the bed, streak through the bars of the gate in the yard like an arrow as he made for the hillside. Now he could only poke a paw beneath the chairs when he lost his spider under them; he got stuck quite regularly, yelling his head off, under the bed; and he could only just squeeze through the bars of the gate.

One day, in fact, I spotted him making his exit through the gate as usual, rushed to retrieve him before he could get into the lane and discovered, to my alarm, that I couldn't get him back. He could obviously squeeze onwards, sliding in the direction of his fur, but he was wedged so tightly otherwise, there was no question of pulling him back.

To let him slip through, on the other hand, meant one victorious swoosh and a game of Seeley at large in the woods. So we opened the gate with Seeley still in it I holding him suspended while Charles nipped quickly through and pulled from the other side – and Father Adams, who was passing by as usual, said 'Another couple of feeds, I reckon, and theest have to saw he out.'

It was quite true. Seeley *was* growing, and he was going to be a very big cat. Already, when they were lying down, it was difficult to tell him from Sheba. But a lot of Seeley's weight was due to his appetite.

Charles said he thought he ate even more than Solomon. 'He couldn't do,' I said, remembering Solomon in his heyday. 'It's such a long time since Solomon was a kitten you must have forgotten his capacity.'

'All I know,' said Charles with firm conviction, 'is that Solomon didn't eat his food before he *got* it.'

That was true, too. Seeley, when he sighted food, would head for it with his tongue already working in and out in anticipation. Hold him back while Sheba ate and you could see him gulping in sympathy. And then, as he watched her, out would come his own tongue. Seeley was eating, too, in imagination.

When it came to eating in practice, his appetite knew no bounds. He would eat his own food, polish off any bits Sheba happened to have left and then look round for more. He would quest the kitchen, nose to the floor, like an otter exploring new territory. (We had seen the *Ring of Bright Water* film, and the resemblance was really remarkable.)

It came perhaps, this zest for food, from being brought up with so many other cats. Eat It Quick And Decide What It Was Later was probably Mum's advice to her young. That, no doubt, was why I found him in the sink one day sampling the washing-up water. And that, no doubt, was why I found him on another occasion – one day when we had visitors, the cooking preparations had been hectic and as usual the kitchen was a welter of pans and dishes – standing on the cooker, his back feet parked in a bowl with an inch of cream in it, while he ecstatically licked the gravy from the grillpan I'd put in the window. Not, I should explain, that he didn't also like cream; presumably standing in it staked his claim to it while he dealt as fast as possible with the gravy.

No wonder he was growing – though, from the size of his feet, he was going to be a lot bigger yet. His whiskers were emerging where he'd singed them, too. I could scarcely believe it. They were growing out like Solomon's. *Spotted...*

He was five months old exactly now and it was almost time for him to be neutered. Around six months was the best time, we knew. I rang to make the appointment. 'You're sure it *is* a male?' the Vet enquired. I said there was no doubt about it.

No doubt about it indeed. 'Fine pair of tonsils he's got, h'ant he?' said Father Adams admiringly one day, unfortunately in the presence of poor Miss Wellington. Miss Wellington, shocked to her very foundations, still turned scarlet when she thought about it.

So there we were, with neutering day coming up, and just then we had some visitors. The two schoolteacher sisters who, in the dark days when we'd lost Solomon, had phoned us with the telephone number that led to Seeley. For weeks we'd been saying they must come and see him, and first there'd been a cat flu scare in the district and we hadn't dared get together, and then it had been Christmas and all of us so busy. Now it was the New Year and over they came to see him. He was absolutely on his best behaviour. Telling them his life history after he'd decided they hadn't come to kidnap him. Rolling on the hearthrug for them. Sitting on their laps. We'd never known our Seeley so attentive.

The sisters had Siamese themselves. Twin seal-point females called Sugar and Spice. Any Siamese owner will recognise it as inevitable as dawn follows dusk that if one of those cats was going down with something, it would be when it or its owners had been in contact with another Siamese.

Sure enough, the very next evening one of the sisters rang up in a panic. Spice was ill, she said. They'd called the Vet. They'd heard that cat-flu was going round in their village. We'd better watch Seeley for symptoms… They'd never forgive themselves if he was ill, she said – but truly, Spice had been positively *bounding* the previous day…

TWELVE

I've no doubt she had. And a short while later she was bounding again though there was one day when she was very, very ill. What she had had, they never knew. Personally he didn't think it *was* cat flu, said the Vet; and her sister, Sugar, hadn't caught it.

Meantime, needless to say, we had our own personal Siamese crisis. Two days after the first phone message I rang to enquire how Spice was getting on. On the road to recovery, thank goodness, said her owner, though the previous day they'd really thought they were going to lose her. 'How's Seeley?' she asked with trepidation. 'Oh, he's absolutely full of beans,' I replied. 'Well, I'm glad you didn't ring yesterday,' she said relievedly. 'We really thought it was cat flu then, and if I'd had to tell you…'

It was inevitable, of course. When I went downstairs next morning, for the first time ever Seeley wasn't sitting on the bureau-top waiting to greet me. He was lying, eyeing me languidly, in his bed before the fire. He was tired, I told myself firmly. And, when he then got up, as strong-looking, apparently, as ever 'Thank goodness for that,' I said. But he didn't come to me. He went to his waterbowl. And if for a moment I was able to dismiss that, too, with Why shouldn't he have a drink – it was natural first thing in the morning – it was soon obvious that something was wrong. He didn't want his breakfast. He kept going back to drink. Eventually – heart-sinkingly – he was sick. Only a very small bilious-looking sick which he then regarded with interest, but we gazed at it as forebodingly as if it were the plague.

Five minutes later, during which time we hit rock-bottom with the conviction that he had cat flu, cheered ourselves up with the fact that Spice had recovered from whatever she'd had and then remembered apprehensively that she almost hadn't, Seeley announced that he felt better. Six minutes later he was eating like a hunter. Ten minutes later he was raucously demanding Out. It had, thank heaven, been a false alarm.

That was what came of drinking dishwater, Charles told him severely. Gosh, he hadn't half felt Ill, said Seeley. Whatever it was, there was one thing we could bet on. We weren't – it was very obvious – going to have a peaceful life with him.

No one who takes on a Siamese ever does, of course. Take the owners of Sugar and Spice. They'd come to see us, some eight months earlier, unhappy because their old dog had died. A poodle, they said, and they felt they could never replace it. Did we think it would be a good idea to have a Siamese cat?

Two Siamese cats, we advised them. Two were much better than one. They kept each other young and were company, particularly when one had to leave them alone. They'd probably be driven mad, we warned them, but they'd never again feel dull. What about their father, who was ninety? they queried doubtfully. It would probably put new life into him, I said, secretly crossing my fingers.

Some months later we received a letter from them. A record of catastrophe, if ever there was one, beginning with one sister's eighty-mile journey to fetch the kittens home. When she got home, to her delight Spice straightaway used an earthbox while she – her name was Dora – stood there in blissful contemplation of her dear little, clean little cat.

She didn't stay blissful for long. Once out of the earthbox – Gosh that was Good, said Spice relievedly – the kitten decided to climb something to celebrate. Straight up the nearest pole she went – which happened to be the leg of Nita, Dora's sister – and Nita departed to her bedroom with laddered nylons, footprinted blouse (Spice just having emerged from the earthbox) and her shoulders furrowed like a ploughfield where Spice had light-heartedly landed. 'Within five minutes of bringing them into the house,' said Dora with awe. And Nita, with equal awe, recalled how she'd gone into her bedroom, prayed for help, and wondered if they could possibly send one back.

All that was in the past, however. Nita was now as devotedly their slave as Dora – which was just as well, since Nita was the one (being at home during the day to look after her father) who had to cope with the situations which the kittens proceeded to develop.

It was Nita, for instance, who had to fetch the Vet when Spice got stuck in the clock. It was a grandfather clock and she crawled in under the bottom and got firmly wedged under the weight. The weight was almost at the bottom and moving steadily downwards; a couple of frantic wriggles and Spice was trapped. First she'd howled, which was simply terrifying, and then she'd gone silent, which was even worse – and Nita couldn't lift the weight for fear of dropping it on her, and was scared of winding up the weight in case Spice was somehow tangled up in it and might come up on the end... By the time the Vet arrived and got her out Spice was stiff and they thought she was dead. She wasn't, though. An injection against shock and she was herself again – though somewhat bruised – within hours. Spice that is, not Nita, who had nightmares about it for days.

Spice was obviously their equivalent of Solomon. Sugar had her one moment of stardom when she got stung by a bee and they thought it was mumps, just as Sheba once, in the days when she was a kitten, had stayed out all night and we thought that a fox had got her. It was Solomon in our case, however, who so regularly got into trouble, and in the case of the sisters it was Spice.

It was Spice who, the day after her spaying operation, was discovered hanging by her front legs from a high branch of a walnut tree, with her back legs waving wildly in the air. So high up they couldn't get at her, said Dora, and they were almost too scared to *look*... Panic-stricken, they rushed out a rolled-up carpet which had just come back from the cleaners and spread it under the tree. Spice thereupon hauled herself up – only just, she made it perfectly obvious

– and went and dangled off a branch that didn't have carpet under it.

It was Spice, too, who climbed all the trellis-work they'd put up round the garden – her one aim, when she'd done it, being to go and sit in the gutter. She was interested in cars, said Dora resignedly; nothing would ever stop her.

If she'd been on a main road, of course, she wouldn't have lasted five minutes. But this was a cul-de-sac and cars went pretty slowly; the main danger was that she might be carried off by accident. Already they'd found her inside their own car bonnet, and there was the time she went missing mysteriously and they'd chased the laundry van...

No, he hadn't seen one like that, said the laundry-man, when they caught him and described the errant Spice. Always putting cats out of the van, though, he was... never knew where they'd got in and all he could do was just to put 'em out...

So they'd looked in all the baskets in the back of his van, called her loudly all the way home in case she'd jumped out and hidden en route... with everybody *looking* at them, said Dora with feeling; especially when they stopped and peered in somebody's garden... And when they got home, of course, there, as they went up the road, was a familiar form waiting for them on the edge of a Gas Board excavation. Been down the Hole in the Road, Spice informed them affably. They been out for a walk or something?

Spice's record might not equal Solomon's yet, but it was obviously going to do so before she finished. Seeley, likewise, was coming up fast in the Solomon stakes. Take dogs, for instance. Solomon's insistence on facing up to dogs in the belief that all of them were afraid of him had led us into some situations at times. He'd frightened poodles and the Rector's Pekinese, been chased through a cloche by a mastiff, and had once been rescued by firemen from the top of a tree.

Spice was pursuing the subject equally intently, what with lording it over a Scottie called Mac and growling ominously at their neighbour's corgi when it passed her in her gutter. These, however, were short-legged dogs. The sisters nearly had a fit when new people moved in across the road, and there, superintending the furniture as it came out of the removal van, was a man holding a greyhound on a leash. 'Oh *no!*' groaned Dora. 'We'll have to *move*,' said Nita. While Spice, shut in, hurled insults at the greyhound through the window.

Eventually, after they'd had several pots of tea to soothe their nerves, the van departed. The man with the greyhound was still in evidence, though – standing at the gate, looking interestedly round the garden. They couldn't go to bed that night, they said, till they'd gone over and enquired of him whether he was the new owner – and when he said No he wasn't; merely a brother-in-law come to help with the move – 'Thank goodness for that!' they'd exclaimed, and apparently he'd looked rather put out.

Now Seeley was on the dog game and we nearly had a fit ourselves when we looked through the window one day and he was out in the roadway, facing up to Jim. Jim was short for Jemima – a fact which was apt to galvanise visitors to the Valley when, as regularly happened, Mrs Penny came panting up the lane behind a huge Labrador on a leash and called, as she passed our gate, 'Isn't it a nuisance? Jim's on heat! It always happens just when I'm busy!'

Short for Jemima or not, Jim didn't half chase the cats and when we saw Seeley out in the lane one day, confronting, like a duellist in the Bois de Boulogne, a Labrador who was grinning back at him from a distance of six feet with the alertness of Red Riding Hood's wolf, we were both of us rooted to the spot. Seeley wore the air of complete unconcern that had been Solomon's wont when he faced up to dogs. He also looked extremely small and Jim, we knew, was so fast...

Recovering ourselves, we shot into the garden. The pair of them were still in the lane, immobile as the combatants in *High Noon*. Jim rolled a merry eye and lolloped her tongue in our direction (actually she was a very friendly dog; she just liked to run after cats); Seeley, in best Wild West tradition, never took his eye from his man.

It was no good trying to get through the gate and pick Seeley up, I muttered to Charles. He'd run, Jim would run after him, heaven knew where the pair of them would finish. And we didn't know yet whether Seeley could climb. If he tried for a tree he might not make it.

Leave it to him, Charles muttered back. And then, 'JIM! HOME!' he rumbled sternly in the deep, imperative voice of Mr Penny.

The command JIM! HOME!', calling the errant one back from chasing cats, horses, other dogs or leaving home to seek her fortune was as familiar a part of the local sound nowadays as was Annabel bawling 'Woohoohoo' or me calling 'Seeley-Weeley-Weeley'. I hadn't realised it was so effective, though. JIM! HOME!' Charles rumbled again – and Jim, tail down, showing the whites of her eyes in our direction (whether with reproach at Charles for hitting below the belt or because she thought it *was* her master and that he was invisibly with us) slunk obediently off down the lane.

The trouble with that, of course, was that Seeley immediately decided he had been the victor. 'I won!' he bawled, following triumphantly after the retreating Jim. 'I made her go home!' And though I fetched him back immediately, informing him that he hadn't won and that it wasn't wise for little cats to say rude things to dogs – thereafter he only had to see a dog, of any size whatever, and he was out through the gate, looking it fearlessly in the eye, informing it that he was Seeley. This was *his* house. Want to dispute it? demanded Seeley belligerently.

Fortunately for him – and due no doubt to the combination of china-white fur, blazing blue eyes and a mask as weird as a badger's – they didn't. One day though, we warned him, they'd work it out that he was only a cat. He wasn't afraid of *them*, said Seeley stoutly.

One thing he was afraid of, however, was horses. Why, we couldn't imagine. He liked Annabel to the extent, now, of sitting between her hooves and you'd have thought he'd regard a horse as being like her, only bigger. To Seeley, however, a horse was a particularly sinister bogey. I did everything I could to accustom him to them... holding him in my arms when one went by (Seeley was away like an eel before the horse had a chance to see him); letting him stand on my shoulder (I still have the scars of that particular take-off); hiding conspiratorially with him in the long grass when one passed below us on the hillside... *I* could stay there if I liked, said Seeley; personally he was going to hide in the middle of the forest.

I was greatly encouraged, therefore, the day someone we knew came up the lane on a hunter and Seeley, instead of fleeing stomach-to-the-ground for cover, watched it come, wide-eyed, but standing his ground determinedly inside the gate.

What about there then? I said, putting him up on the gatepost where he would, I thought, feel safer than on the ground and could view the intruder with nose-to-nose equality. Up here was even better, said Seeley, climbing for the first time ever from the gatepost on to the adjoining coalhouse roof. And so it was, of course; it was Sheba's favourite vantage point and many an adversary Solomon had sworn at from up there, too – though in times of definite danger he'd preferred the still higher roof of the woodshed.

So, vastly pleased at this fresh step in the direction I wanted (Solomon had always liked horses and now Seeley, it seemed, was beginning to take an interest), I awaited the arrival of the rider and we began to exchange local news. 'The new boy?' I said... 'Oh, he's right here on the roof. Don't look as if you've noticed him, though – he's just getting used to horses'...

If she'd passed by in the middle of the lane it would probably have been all right. Seeley on the roof under the lilac branches would have felt secure, and confidently in ambush. But we were talking at the gate and the horse, growing bored, decided to look around. He was sixteen hands high and his nose was right by the coalhouse roof. His ears went forward with interest when he saw Seeley sitting on it and he stretched out his head, very cautiously, for a further, closer, look.

I, concentrating on the horse, was saying 'Seeley – come and meet Major' – never dreaming that Seeley could feel unsafe. It was the rider, facing inwards, who saw what was going on – and she was so paralysed with horror, all that happened was that her eyes grew round. Catching the direction of her gaze, I swung round just in time to see the end of it. Seeley, frightened beyond measure by this close-up view of the monster, wasn't scrambling down the coalhouse wall as most cats would have done. Deciding, it seemed, that distance was his only hope Seeley had jumped straight out off the coalhouse roof as if suddenly provided with wings. When I saw him he was actually sailing through the air – before, with a horribly resounding smack, he landed out in the middle of the yard, scrambled up and went on running.

He wasn't hurt. He was large enough now not to be a tiny, fragile kitten – yet young enough, on the other hand, to take such an impact in his stride. Things were running true to form, said Charles reflectively later that evening. Solomon had jumped out of the bedroom window once and landed in a hydrangea, and now Seeley, following suit, had jumped off the coalhouse roof...

Running true to form my foot, I said weakly. I hadn't been so scared in years. Seeley mightn't have lost one of his nine lives – but by gum, I'd lost one of mine!

THIRTEEN

Things were running true to form all right. It wasn't long before Seeley – who, after all, had never seen a horse before he came to us and animals as big as that took a little getting used to – was out there, just as Solomon had been, trotting happily up the Forestry trail in the wake of the riding school, while I dropped everything and hared after him.

He went even further than that. Major appeared with his owner, Miss Howland, one day, with a boxer running beside him. Miss Howland having stopped for a chat, I was never more surprised in my life than when Seeley stepped out through the bars of the gate over which we were talking and sat boldly in the road in front of Major. Like to be Friends? said Seeley, gazing manfully up at the horse. Didn't mind if he Did, said Major, putting his nose down to within an inch of him.

At that moment up came the boxer. Miss Howland said he was fond of cats, so we didn't whisk Seeley in again with our usual admonition about being careful – and the boxer wagged his bottom at Seeley and Seeley tried to look like a boxer back. It would undoubtedly result in his being more familiar with dogs than ever, I said, but it was worth it for just this moment. A horse, a dog and a kitten, communing happily in a quiet country lane. A moment out of Paradise, when surely even the angels must have smiled...

Not for long, however. Looming ominously on the horizon was Seeley's trip to the Vet, and if the angels had heard him on that little lot, I reckon they'd have covered their ears in horror.

He should actually have had the operation weeks before, but we'd put it off. First, after Spice's illness, to make sure he didn't go down with anything himself, and then, to be perfectly truthful, because I hated taking a fit, bouncing kitten to the Vet. Sugieh, our first Siamese – Solomon and Sheba's mother – had died as the result of being spayed. Neutering a male is much, much simpler of course. Even with spaying, nowadays, there is nothing whatsoever to worry about. Sheba, when she was spayed, was playing unconcernedly the very next day...

All the same, remembering Sugieh I worried about it. About his having an anaesthetic. About his going without food beforehand (he got all tragic if he just had to wait while his fish cooked; Hamlet wouldn't be in it if he had to miss a couple of meals). About the sorry, frightened little kitten we'd take home afterwards – and we'd hate ourselves for days, I had no doubt.

It had to be done, though. He was over six months old. Any moment now those innocently enquiring explorations into the pine trees might turn into swashbuckling, long-distance forays after the girls. He was already beginning to show significant interest in Sheba – pursuing her with excited 'Mrrr-mrrr-mrrrs' and jumping embarrassingly on her neck.

'Dear little man,' beamed Miss Wellington innocently. 'Isn't it nice to see how well he gets on with her?' A little too well in our opinion; so we booked him up at the Vet's for three o'clock one afternoon, kept him without food by dint of shutting him in our bedroom – putting Sheba up there to keep him company after we'd fed her secretly in the kitchen – and just after two-thirty, ignoring his protests about being Weak and Faint with Hunger; wherever it was he was going we'd be lucky if he Got There Alive... the procession set forth.

Just after three-thirty it was back again. It could only have happened to us. Knowing full well how germs can be floating about in waiting rooms – and Siamese, as we also knew full well, are particularly susceptible to germs – I'd left Seeley, in Sheba's basket, in the car with Charles and had gone in myself to wait our turn. There were two people there before me. A man with a dog, and a woman with a tabby cat in an open shopping basket. The cat lay listless and very quiet on its blanket. 'What's wrong with it?' I asked the owner – and knew the answer even before I got it. 'Cat flu,' she answered worriedly. 'At least, I think it is.'

It was, too. The Vet, swabbing down his table when she'd gone, said this was the second case today and we'd better take Seeley home again. 'Leave it for another month or so,' he said. 'Till we're sure that this is over.'

'This' was the pulmonary type of cat flu. Against the more serious enteric variety there is, of course, a vaccine, and Seeley had been inoculated, as had Solomon and Sheba. Against the pulmonary variety there is as yet no vaccine, however – and though, said the Vet, most ordinary cats recover from it (just a couple of days' heavy cold, he said, and then they're right as rain) Siamese are often very ill.

Thanking our lucky stars we hadn't taken Seeley into the waiting room, we turned our tracks for home. It was the only thing we could thank our lucky stars for, though. Seeley had kicked up enough fuss on the outward journey – shouting, screaming, chewing piece after piece off the basket. He was supposed not to have anything in his stomach, I wailed. It would be even *worse* if he filled it up with wickerwork. 'Why don't you stop him, then?' said Charles, trying hard to concentrate on the winding road. He should try poking *his* fingers in, I said. I'd almost lost a couple already.

On the way home he surpassed himself, however. INCARCERATED! he roared at the passing cars in a voice so raucous Charles said it certainly *was* time he was neutered. DELIBERATELY STARVED! he announced with a pathos that would have done credit to Irving. BEEN IN HERE FOR HOURS AND I HAVEN'T HAD MY BREAKFAST! he informed the garage attendant when we stopped for petrol. Heaven help us when we took him down to Halstock, said Charles. Forty miles of this and we'd be lucky to have a car…

We got him home, whisked him out fast and gave him some food. All in one Piece still, he informed Sheba happily

Really, of course, the locals did know what was going on – just as, after a day or two of surreptitious enquiry, they knew what our frost coverings were for, though they might pretend they didn't. It was strangers to the place who were genuinely puzzled – and not only by the drapings, either.

'Well, I'm glad I asked' said one passing walker when I'd explained about the frost covers and the schoolhouse roof. I thought they had some connection... And what about that sledge dog up the hill that pulls the pram? Did they get him from Alaska or something?'

There was an explanation for that, too. The Darlings, who owned the Samoyed, were merely putting him to the breed's original use. He'd inherited an obvious liking for pulling things, they said. Why push the pram when Rob was willing to pull?

Meanwhile, while people were speculating about the schoolhouse roof and the frost covers and a dog apparently practising for the Arctic, I was spending long periods on the hillside behind the cottage. I had discovered that if I sat down somewhere and didn't chase after him, Seeley, who was becoming increasingly fond of me, would play around within contact distance – which meant that while I watched him we had some peace of mind.

It was very pleasant watching him, too. It was becoming warmer now and this was Seeley's first spring. The exuberance with which he chased the butterflies, the wonder with which he regarded the birds, the joy with which he rolled and thrust his paws at me through the grass – I shared it with him, this heaven that he was discovering daily. This was the place to be, he said. He was glad that he lived with us.

as he ate. He was indeed, and for the next few weeks it meant we not only had to watch him with Sheba (she didn't like being jumped on and occasionally there was a noisy free-for-all) but we had to keep a weather eye on Seeley to make sure that he didn't wander off.

This – seeing there was no guarantee once he vanished into the pinewoods that he was going to reappear again on the same side – led to all sorts of preventive manoeuvres. Frantic round-ups during which we ran about the lane and hillside like ants; standing over him while he dug holes in the garden because he was particularly likely to streak off as if jet-propelled after that; doing my imitation of a prowling tomcat which, for a while, infallibly brought him back...

At first I'd tried imitating a dog but, as with Solomon and Sheba when they were young, that hadn't been very successful. Standing in a lane barking 'Row-row-row' at a completely empty hillside is not the best way of impressing fellow humans with one's sanity, either. I got some pretty peculiar looks from passers-by.

I got some pretty peculiar ones when I did my cat imitations, come to that. 'Mrrrrow!... meeaOOOW... RaaaaAAAAH!' I would wail impassionedly while Charles peered anxiously up the Forestry lane. This – performed outside the back gate and followed by a sand-dance shuffle and clapping of hands which was supposed, for Seeley's benefit, to be me chasing the tomcat and indignantly shooing him off – was enough to transfix anybody who heard it, and though I always looked to see that the coast was clear before I started, the lanes in our part of the world are very winding and somebody was always catching up with me in the middle.

On one occasion it was Major and Miss Howland. She was transfixed all right. Even more so, she informed me afterwards, when out of the woods and down the hillside, flat on his stomach like an otter, came a homing Siamese cat. He was growling sinisterly to himself as he slipped in through the gate. What on earth, she wanted to know, were we going to think of next?

It wasn't so much a case of thinking of things as of necessity leading to invention. After a week or so of my only having to imitate a tomcat to bring him home as if by magic, for instance, Seeley got wise to the fact that it was me. Either that or he decided he was bigger now so he'd go looking for the cat who did it. At any rate, any time I did my imitations now he took no notice whatsoever – and if I wanted him in because we were going out, he proceeded determinedly, with his ears flat to show he couldn't hear, in the opposite direction. Thus it was, one morning when I was going riding and the horses would be ready at ten o'clock, that Seeley decided this was the morning when *he* was going exploring. In the Woods, he said, mounting steadily up the hillside ahead of me. Not Going To, he said when I pleaded with him to come back. That was only for Babies, he said when I desperately did my tomcat call. And, to show what he thought of that ruse, he did a sudden exuberant caper into the trees.

I did an equally speedy caper after him. It was half past nine now and if I lost sight of him, as well I knew, he wouldn't come out again for ages. He began to saunter beneath the tall, dark groves of the pine trees. Oh Lord, I thought, despairingly; we could go for miles like this. He did a light-hearted sortie or two up passing tree trunks. My gosh, I thought; if he goes right to the top...

He didn't. Like Solomon, Seeley couldn't climb for toffee. Three feet up and off he'd plop, pretending that wasn't the one he'd meant to go up after all. Neither was the next one, he said. He was only showing me how he could very well if he wanted to. He then light-heartedly poked a paw down a mouse hole in the pine needles before darting tantalisingly behind another tree a few feet ahead.

I hope the mouse forgave me. The only way I stopped Seeley from prancing off still further was to seize a dried-up bracken stem and poke it feverishly down the mouse hole myself. 'Look Seeley,' I said ingratiatingly, demonstrating that the stem would go inches and inches in and then, when you withdrew it, come inches and inches out...

It stopped him going any further but it didn't entice him back within grabbing distance. I finally achieved that by lying flat on my back, pretending to be dead, and crying. 'Woohoohoo,' I wept softly with one half-opened eye on Seeley. 'Oh, Woohoohoohoohoo...' Whereupon Seeley, who apparently did care for me a little, came – albeit non-chalantly – back, walked heavily across my stomach, and went on to sniff a plant beneath the nearest tree. Raising myself up stealthily I grabbed his tail. Seeley jumped yards on the end of it – and I jumped yards myself when, from just behind me, a frightened voice said 'Oh dear dear me... I really thought you'd been thrown!' It was Miss Wellington. Intent on capturing Seeley I hadn't heard her coming down the track – and she, intent on gathering pine cones, had apparently nearly dropped herself when she saw me, wearing riding clothes, lying flat under a tree on my back.

I told her what I'd been doing. Miss Wellington, who was odd herself, was about the only one to whom I could have explained such a manoeuvre and not have been thought dotty. 'What a good idea,' she said admiringly. 'I must try it myself when Sooty won't come in.'

I made my excuses, carted Seeley back to the cottage – by now it was five minutes to ten – and made it to the riding stables by the skin of my teeth. It was time, I said to Charles that night, that Seeley really was done. I was beginning to have nightmares about his roaming off through the forest.

So we fixed it up again and once more the expedition set forth. There was a difference this time in that Seeley, now two months older than on his first abortive trip, was so much bigger that he wouldn't fit into Sheba's basket and we'd had to buy him a new one. We'd got him one of the kind that looks like a cage, with a dome-topped wickerwork body and a complete wire door as the front. We'd been told that cats who dislike travelling – as had Solomon in the first place and now, indomitably following him, the vociferous Seeley – sometimes change their attitude completely if they travel in something they can see out of.

So we'd bought this basket, which was big enough for a dog kennel (better get a large one while we were at it, said Charles: we didn't know how much Seeley was going to grow) and in it, on the back seat, sat Seeley, like a little black-faced pea in an enormous wickerwork pod.

I hated to see him in it. Seeley hated it, too – but not so much, quite definitely, as in a closed-in basket he couldn't see out of. I could get my fingers through the wire bars, too, and thus – letting him chew my fingers instead of the wickerwork, and we hadn't put a blanket in the basket so he couldn't eat that – we got him safely to the Vet with an empty stomach. We had a morning appointment this time; a special concession so he wouldn't have to miss his breakfast *and* his lunch. And the cat flu epidemic was over, and it was a fine warm day so he wouldn't catch cold.

The one thing we would have done if we'd had time was put another couple of straps on the basket. There was only one at the moment, half-way up the wire door. It needed at least two more to guarantee the basket entirely Seeley-proof. It was all right just this once, though, we decided. We'd be with him till he was handed over to the Vet. After his operation he'd be too wobbly to think of escaping. That was the reason we'd bought the basket so hurriedly – to give him plenty of room to lie out in when he was coming round.

So we delivered him to the Vet who told us to come back again just before lunch. If Seeley had recovered consciousness by then, he said, we could take him home. He was definitely taking no chances, however. If he wasn't round, we must wait till the afternoon.

He took no chances to the extent that, noting that there was only one strap on our basket and knowing Siamese potentialities even better than we did, when he'd done the operation he put Seeley into a cage. A white-barred affair with an outside fastening from which there was no possible chance of escape.

Not until someone opened the door, that is. When we went back just before lunch the assistant said would we please take a seat in the waiting room; she'd see if he'd come round yet. Awed by her white-starched overall and air of efficiency we did so – and were out of our chairs like rockets when a few seconds later (gone was the brisk efficiency now, and she was clutching one bleeding hand with the other) she returned to say could we please come at once. Our little Siamese had escaped.

In theory Seeley should have been still extremely dopey and easily transferred to his basket. In practice, he was conscious and hopping mad. When she'd opened the cage to get him out he'd scratched her and dashed into the dispensary. He wouldn't let her get near him, she said, and he was growling at her really horribly.

If ever our hearts went out to our New Boy it was in the moment when we saw him at bay in the corner of that dispensary – groggy still from the effects of the anaesthetic, but determined to fight to the death. I called to him, and he stopped growling at once, and let Charles and me, between us, pick him up.

Feeling absolute heels – it was nobody's fault that he'd escaped but it must have been a terrible experience for him, coming round in a strange cage like that and thinking his friends had deserted him – we took him home. He was Hungry, he said when we got indoors, so we gave him a plateful of rabbit. He'd been Fighting People he informed Sheba through mouthfuls of food when he saw her. Obviously the operation itself hadn't troubled him a bit.

If we thought that was going to be the end of his wanderings, however, we were very much mistaken. Two days later he went missing and, when we did catch up with him, for the first time ever he wasn't in the woods, but coming back jauntily down the road.

I thought his operation was supposed to stop all that, I said, going out to usher him sternly through the gate. That was only for Girls, said Seeley as he marched importantly in. Now he didn't have them on his mind any more, he could concentrate on being an explorer.

FOURTEEN

He did too, just as Solomon had done before him. I remember, when Solomon was that age, building a low stone wall along one side of the front path, and so often did I check to see where Solomon was while I was doing it – and every time I checked I had to down tools to fetch him back – that the wall, when it was finished, had bends in it like the Serpentine.

I wasn't building a wall now but I was trying to dig the flowerbeds, the procedure usually being – one forkful, Seeley was on the path; two forkfuls, Seeley was still on the path; three forkfuls, Seeley was *still* on the path; four forkfuls, Seeley was suddenly gone. Transported by means of levitation, apparently, since one never saw him going. Just one moment he was there and the next he was high on the hillside heading for the forest, fifty yards up the lane making for the village – or, more often than not, nowhere in sight at all and we didn't know which way he'd gone.

'We'll have to put up that cage,' we kept saying – but it was early yet. Only February. Too cold for a little cat to sit in the open in a cage. So I alternated between digging the flowerbeds and running to fetch back Seeley (Seeley was definitely my cat, said Charles; he wouldn't come to him) while Charles got busy on his fruit trees.

This year, he said, he was *determined* to have some fruit – to which end (as, being in a valley, we are particularly susceptible to frost) he set about protecting the early-blooming pear trees. He started by covering them with some old lace curtains; relics of my grandmother's, which my Aunt Louisa had given us. He continued – getting really enthusiastic about this frost protection now and there weren't enough curtains to go round – by using large hessian sacks which he bought up by the dozens. Charles being an artistic type who doesn't worry too much about the appearance of things, the result was that that spring visitors to the Valley (and any residents, too, who hadn't been past for a while) were positively electrified by the sight of our orchard, which looked as though it had been taken over by a convocation of monks, about ten feet tall, wearing white lace cassocks surmounted by sinisterly hooded habits.

They had this pointed-hood appearance because Charles, to keep the hessian from touching the blossom, had one corner of each huge sack propped high above its tree on a cane. A simple and, if one knew it, a perfectly reasonable explanation, but as usual few people did. As usual, too, in a country village, people put their own interpretations upon the phenomenon.

'Scarecrows,' I heard one old man inform another as they stood at the orchard gate and stared. 'Oh ah,' said his companion placidly, as though thirty-odd scarecrows to an acre was nothing at all unusual. 'Put there to keep the cats off was another knowledgeable verdict. (Though we hadn't come to that yet, even with Seeley.) 'Bet they frightens the horses,' said somebody else. 'Looks like a lot of witches,' said another. ''Ouldn't like to come across they in the dark unbeknownst,' said a further voice going past in the dusk.

By moonlight, in fact, with the frost glittering on them, they did look rather spooky. 'Minds I,' said Father Adams, who'd seen them himself one night en route to the Rose and Crown 'of Fred Ferry's father and the ghost in the churchyard.'

We didn't know there was a churchyard ghost, we said. Nor there weren't, said Father Adams, proceeding to tell us the tale.

It seemed that years before, Fred Ferry's father, whose name was also Fred, had been renowned for getting rolling drunk and then going and sitting on a stone in the churchyard, moaning to himself about being such a sinner. 'Used to frighten all the women coming home from the Mother's Meeting,' said Father Adams. 'Didn't matter that they knowed 'twas he. The noise he made did always put the wind up 'em.' So the other men decided to teach old Fred a lesson and one night, when there was to be a funeral the following day, one of them got down into the newly dug grave just after closing time while the rest hid behind the adjoining headstones.

'Along comes Old Fred,' said Father Adams. 'A-moaning and a-blathering about this business of being a sinner, and up rises Tom in an old white sheet and calls on'n to repent.'

'And did it work?' I asked Father Adams. 'Naw,' he said reminiscently, 'but 'twere nearly the end of Tom. Old Fred, thinking 'twere a ghost, picked up the sexton's spade and hit 'n on the head. 'Get back down there, you b.' he shouted. 'Stay down where theest belong!'

I thought of the story every time I saw the frost covers in the dusk after that. At the top of the hill, in the village, too, another mysterious erection had suddenly appeared. They were putting a new roof on the old schoolhouse – a building long turned over to private occupation. The local children went to school now in the adjoining village.

The surrounding cottages were very small, like ours. But the schoolhouse towered over them to about twice their height, and when the builders had put scaffolding all round it they covered the house with a complete tarpaulin roof and then – on account of this is high-up hill country and the wind through the scaffolding was rather fierce – they lashed tarpaulins all round the sides of the scaffolding as well. Inside this the men worked, made their tea on a plank about thirty feet up and were, from the sound of it, ecstatically happy.

From the outside, however, this enormous tarpaulined cube presented another focal point for speculation. Some wits decided there was a statue going up under it. 'Dam' gert bloke then... p'raps 'tis a group of 'em' said one onlooker, following which rumours of the Parish Council being done in stone were rife in the Rose and Crown. 'Putting up a supermarket' said another – and from the size of the tarpaulin casing, that could have been possible too.

We were glad too, though we certainly needed our wits about us. One day, for instance, when for once I wasn't trailing him, Seeley vanished completely. We searched, we called him, I did my cat imitations – Seeley didn't answer. 'He's up on the hillside somewhere,' said Charles. 'I saw him going in that direction.' So, keeping a weather eye on the hillside where the grass was now so long we couldn't possibly find him unless he decided to cooperate, we continued – albeit anxiously – with our gardening.

It was a little while later that I heard squawking and, looking up, saw a magpie advancing in determined hops through the grass. One of a pair that were friendly with Annabel, and often pecked round her while she grazed. 'Got his eye on something,' I thought, and went on weeding. Until, a second or two afterwards, I saw the second magpie hopping through the grass from another direction and, dropping my trowel, I shouted and started to run.

I was right. It was Seeley they were after. He was there in the grass just beyond them. Whether they were playing with him or whether, which was more likely, he'd been stalking them and they were out to teach him a lesson – either way it was a good thing I'd been watching for him. I'd heard of magpies attacking cats before… One deliberately attracting the cat's attention, while the other crept up from behind.

He was very subdued when I carried him back, lying as inconspicuously as he could in my arms, his eyes as round as an owl's, his ears so flat he looked practically streamlined. Wasn't going out Again, he announced – which was how he came to discover the little fish.

We'd hatched them ourselves the previous year. After the flood, as a result of giving them the fresh supply of water, our goldfish had started spawning like mad. Usually they ate the eggs as soon as they laid them but this time, by way of experiment, I took some out with a teaspoon and put them into teacups to hatch. Teacups without handles, of which we have rather a lot, and it needs shallow water to hatch them out.

They looked like tiny, transparent pinheads – with, after a day or two, a little black dot inside them which showed they were fertile. According to the book they should have taken from four days to a fortnight to hatch, depending on the weather – but the summer was very cold that year and when, after nearly a fortnight, they still showed no signs of emerging, I tried putting them in warmer water.

The result was miraculous. Those fish were out within *seconds*. One moment there was a tiny little globule with what now looked like an eyelash in it – and the next the egg was rolling emptily on the bottom of the teacup while the eyelash was out, clinging prehensilely to the side. For days we had a row of teacups with static black eyelashes in them in the kitchen window – and then the eyelashes began to swim, and developed two little eyes, and eventually, unbelievably, they became tiny transparent fish.

We hatched more than fifty, but the mortality rate among goldfish fry is very high. If one saves ten per cent one is lucky, so we were just about right when we finished up with five. We kept them, during the winter, in a plastic bowl on top of the kitchen cupboard; they were too small yet for the big pond, where their relations would promptly have eaten them, and it was too cold to leave them out of doors on their own.

Charles thought a lot of those fish. He took them down regularly to change the water, feed them and admire them. Marvellous little chaps they were, he assured them; he was going to build them a new pond all to themselves. Actually there was very nearly no need to. The same night that Seeley was stalked by the magpies, Seeley in turn found the fish. On the kitchen table, where Charles had left them while he came in to have his supper, and where, when we went out, Seeley was happily fishing.

He was standing with one front foot actually *in* the bowl of fish and the other paw poised to strike. He hadn't caught any yet – though the fishing paw was wet and had obviously been in the water pretty often – and he couldn't understand why we yelled and grabbed him. Spoiling all his Fun, he wailed as I bore him away. Didn't like him doing Anything. Bet we were in league with those silly old Magpies.

From then on we had to keep a wire cake-tray permanently on top of the fish bowl, remember never to leave it on the table, and keep a watchful eye on the cupboard to make sure Seeley hadn't found a way of climbing up it. This was indoors. As at the same time we had to make sure he wasn't chasing Sheba – and, if outdoors, that he wasn't wandering off or stalking bees, life, like the weather, was certainly warming up.

The qualms I'd had about our own bees had happily resolved themselves. Charles had gone up early in the year to see if they needed feeding and found that they just weren't there. The most likely explanation, seeing that there were no dead bees in the hive and all the honey had gone, was that the bees from one of the stranger hives up the Valley had come on a raiding expedition, as bees sometimes do if they are close to a weakened hive, and that – as again has been known to happen – our bees, instead of fighting them, had matily gone off to join them taking their honey stores with them.

It was the best thing that could have happened in the circumstances. There were the bees up the Valley to pollinate Charles's fruit trees. Charles wasn't likely to be stung any more, with the other hives so far away. Seeley – I sighed with relief – was never likely to come across a hive at all. Not one with bees in it, anyway, though our own hive still stood empty on the hill.

'Better get he down fast,' advised Father Adams. 'Afore the bees swarms further up and comes back down here to live.' There wasn't much fear of that, however. The man who kept the other bees was an expert.

We had to watch Seeley with the ordinary bees around the garden, but there were nothing like as many as there would have been. Seeley, of course, never having seen a bee before, was absolutely entranced to have so many exciting playmates. He stalked them on his stomach, he leapt after them through the air, he flattened all the crocuses making frustrated pounces.

The main thing was to stop him picking one up in his mouth. If one stung him on the paw he'd learn to leave them alone, but a sting in the mouth can be dangerous. Olive oil was the best quick first aid if that happened, I'd read – applied with a feather if the bee-sting was in the throat. So I kept a feather and the oil-bottle handy, hoped I'd never have to use it, and meanwhile kept on running. Out to fetch him back from the lane. Up to fetch him back from the hillside. Out once more because he was now after a bee – a bumble-bee this time, and it was slower and he almost caught it.

Didn't want him to have any fun at All, wailed Seeley as I carted him back to where I was weeding a border. It wasn't that. It was that I wanted to know he was safe. In the end all our precautions were in vain, however. Seeley was bitten by an adder.

FIFTEEN

He met up with it in Annabel's field, behind the cottage. The one place we'd thought, since she patrolled it so solidly and the grass was down to billiard-table level, was completely adder-free. Charles actually saw it happen, though he didn't know then that it was an adder. He was cementing a gatepost; I was mowing the lawn; we were keeping an eye open for Seeley who we knew was up there somewhere.

It was Charles who saw him come out of the trees at the top of her field, amble a few yards down one of the paths and then crouch, flatten his ears and pounce at something. A bee, Charles thought at the time – but we weren't so worried about bees now, seeing that Seeley hadn't so far managed to catch one.

A moment or two later he said he could hear a cat crying and where was Sheba? Indoors, I said. I couldn't hear the crying myself on account of the noise of the mower. And then Charles said suddenly 'Quick – it's Seeley!' and was in the lane and up the hillside like a flash.

Seeley tried to walk to him but could only stumble. And all the time we could hear this dreadful crying.

He was still crying – crying with every breath he took in a frightening monotone – when Charles got him down to me at the gate. His paw was already huge and there was something that looked like water oozing from it. We carried him in and put him on the table, hoping against hope it might be a bee-sting. Seeley couldn't stand up by now and still he was crying, crying, crying. My own heart nearly stopped beating. I said 'Oh my goodness… it's an adder!'

Somehow we telephoned the Vet. Get him over as fast as we could, he said; it was quicker for us to go to him than for him to come to us; he'd have everything ready at the surgery. Somehow we got the car out, and Seeley into his basket, and were speeding up the hill. We hadn't stopped for anything. We were still in our old gardening clothes. I hadn't even washed my hands; they were covered in earth.

Halfway to the surgery Seeley suddenly quietened. He was looking at me with big round eyes but he didn't appear to be quite so frightened. 'I bet it was a bee-sting after all,' I said, 'and we've been making all this fuss for nothing.'

The Vet didn't think so. 'That's pretty big for a bee-sting,' he said, examining a paw which was now swollen up to Seeley's shoulder. And when I said but wouldn't Seeley have been unconscious by now if it really had been an adder, he said not necessarily. In his experience, he said, cats and dogs had more resistance to adder-bite than was generally supposed. Some did die within a very short time – if, for instance, they were bitten on the mouth; but if they were bitten in the foot, like Seeley, he'd known a good many of them to recover. It was shock we had to guard against, he said. It was half an hour now since Seeley'd been bitten and he hadn't yet collapsed. He'd give him a cortisone injection and we'd keep our fingers crossed. Take him home; bathe, bathe and keep on bathing his paw in water as hot as he could stand it – and if Seeley did collapse we were to call him at once.

Seeley didn't collapse – though, when we got him home and out of his basket and I saw the size of his leg, I was pretty near it myself. He wouldn't have his paw bathed, either. It Hurt, he said, and rushed to hide under the table. So – not knowing whether we were doing right but remembering that with adder-bite in humans one is supposed to keep the patient still to prevent the venom circulating – we abandoned that and put him on our bed, in his favourite refuge, the nest of sweaters, with a hot-water bottle in it to keep him warm.

Years before, Sheba had had a swollen paw and we thought it might have been an adder and the Vet had given her antihistamine. They didn't give antihistamine now, he'd explained in the surgery; some cats reacted to it badly. They didn't give snake-serum, either. Some cats reacted to that. They'd found it best to treat them for shock.

All I knew, looking at Seeley lying quiet against the bottle, his paw stretched out before him like a furry black bolster, was that Sheba's paw had never swollen like that. Huge it was now, and when I touched his shoulder he cried. Either Sheba's bite hadn't been from an adder – or was cortisone enough?

It was. Our Vet, as usual, knew what he was doing. Seeley's leg was so swollen that at one time it must have been at least four times its normal diameter. It couldn't *get* any bigger without bursting, I said, looking at it despairingly. But Seeley didn't collapse. When, at three in the morning, we got up to see how he was, he was sitting up himself, looking at us alertly, and we could see the shape of his leg. It was still badly swollen, and the paw on the end of it was gross, but at least it didn't look so much like a policeman's truncheon.

By midday it was down still further. By evening he could walk on it – though still with a decided limp. We ourselves were still shaken by the narrow squeak he'd had. 'No more putting it off,' said Charles. 'We'd better build that cage.'

We did. We also, for Annabel's sake, scoured her field for signs of the adder, but we couldn't find it. How was it *she'd* never trodden on one if they were up there? I asked. Because of the ground vibration when she walked, said Charles; an adder would hear her coming and slip away before she reached it, but Seeley's light little tread wouldn't have disturbed it at all. The water from Seeley's paw – that, said the Vet, had been serum; the liquid that is left when blood coagulates. We hadn't seen that with Sheba, as we realized when we thought about it. There wasn't much doubt that Seeley had crossed swords with an adder.

So we erected his cage. A temporary one, said Charles; he'd put it up properly later. The main thing, at the moment, was to get some protection up fast.

It was – as it needs to be with a Siamese – a big cage, about twelve feet by six, and five feet high, consisting of four iron stakes sunk into the lawn with inch-mesh wire netting fixed round it. The final cage would also have a wire netting roof, but that needed crossbars to support it. For the moment, until we had time to make the crossbars, we covered it with one of Charles's fruit nets. An unbreakable nylon one, of which he'd just bought several dozens to replace the frost coverings. The frost danger was over, Charles had reported, but now the blasted birds were at the blossom…

And how they were! Bullfinches, blue tits, wood pigeons – they were up in the orchard in droves. The wood pigeons only attacked the cherry trees, but the small birds were everywhere at once. They'd never seen such blossom, obviously, thanks to Charles's frost coverings which had protected it. That – putting up the nets; sometimes several nets to a tree if it was a large one and it *had* to be done, said Charles; several of the trees were already completely stripped – was why Seeley's adder cage was only a temporary one. Charles needed all his time to put up the nets.

So I draped the fruit net roof over the cage myself, tying it every few inches with string, and put Seeley inside for a try out. He protested immediately. INCARCERATED! SEND FOR THE POLICE! CLAUSTROPHOBIA! he roared, sitting bolt upright inside the wire and proceeding to bawl his head off.

He couldn't get out, though. We'd fixed the bottom wire down with tent pegs and, inspect it though he might, he couldn't pull that up. He wasn't going to be in it permanently, of course. Just for an hour or so when there might be adders about, when it was a shame to shut him indoors but we didn't have time to watch him.

All was well the first day. Thought he was going to be shut in there For Ever, he complained when I let him out again, but it didn't seem to have worried him overmuch. All seemed well the second day, too. Seeley was in his cage; Sheba, who liked it really warm, was sleeping in the car; I, with tranquillity of mind at last, was getting on with some writing. Tranquillity as to where he was, that is, not tranquillity as far as sound went, since Seeley, for nearly an hour, had been howling with every breath. At last all was peaceful, however. He was getting used to it at last, I thought – and looked up, right at that moment, to find him sitting triumphantly on the floor beside me.

He'd climbed the wire adjoining one of the corner poles, where it was taut, and, while clinging to it, had pushed his way out under the net. That we could tell from the turned-back piece of fruit netting. So I ran string through the netting on the corner as if I were sewing it; congratulated myself next day, when I saw his little bullet-head thrusting vainly against the roof while he clung to the wire like a monkey, that I'd foiled *that* attempt at a breakthrough – and half an hour later, looking out through the window from my typewriter, there he was proceeding across the lawn. Got out through the Other Corner, he announced triumphantly when he saw me. And sure enough, when I went out, the fruit netting was pushed back by the other pole.

At least, I thought, firmly lacing up that escape hatch, he wouldn't try getting out through the back. He wouldn't realize it was *possible* to get out through there. At his age he couldn't have that much intelligence. He had, though. Twice more he emerged like a little black Houdini, until I'd laced down all four corners and, for good measure, all round the sides as well.

Now he couldn't get out. In fact, as the weather was warmer we put Sheba in with him for company and he didn't want to get out. They had a rug in there, their water bowl, a plate of food and an earthbox (the latter two to meet Seeley's requirements) and at last we had some peace. People spotted the cage through the trees and began to speculate, of course. 'Wonder what they got in there?' said one. 'Looks like they'm keeping rabbits now,' said another. 'That's to stop the new one from getting bitten,' said somebody else who'd obviously heard about the adder.

Miss Wellington had heard about it, too. She was now going around in slacks. 'On account of the snakes,' she told the postman. And though there was no reason why she shouldn't wear slacks – people much older than she wore them nowadays, though not usually in psychedelic pink – villages being what they are, and Miss Wellington having hitherto been seen only in long tweed skirts except in high summer when she wore long and drooping voiles, there was certainly some excitement over that.

'They old snakes'd better watch out or they'll die of shock when they sees she,' opined Fred Ferry. 'Got her eye on old Bill Porter, I reckons,' said Father Adams – Bill Porter being a widower and well over eighty. 'Not if I sees she first,' said Bill Porter when they chaffed him, while Miss Wellington tripped skittishly in her slacks among her toadstools.

We, meanwhile, having solved the problem of keeping Seeley safe for a guaranteed hour or two a day, still had to keep watch on him when he wasn't in the cage. He couldn't be locked up all the time. He had to have his periods of freedom. And have such periods he did, while I walked with him in the Forestry lane, sat patiently near him while he investigated the hedgerows and played happy games of tag with him in the grass.

'He ought to learn to stay in the garden sometimes though,' said Charles. 'Not be like Solomon; always out through the gate.' So the next thing that appeared on the lawn was a permanent pile of peasticks, and I excavated the clock golf hole.

The peasticks were an accident. Charles, having pruned some of the branches off the nut tree by the coalhouse, left them in a pile on the lawn until he had time to move them (he just *had* to get on with putting up the nets, he said; those birds weren't going to beat him) and there Seeley found them and said they made a super ambush. As he could be guaranteed to stay under them for at least twenty minutes after he was first let out in the morning (spying on the birds, leaping out at the bees, and occasionally landing on Sheba) it was obviously worth leaving them there. There they still remain, too, though now they have been there for months, with a little cat lurking under them and people wondering why we haven't moved them.

The clock golf hole was deliberate. Solomon, when he was young, had been very fond of clock golf. It kept him on the lawn for ages – one of us putting the ball while Solomon either chased it, tail high, across the grass, or practically stood on his head in the hole. He liked it so much that once, when a visitor mislaid her car keys, at a time when Solomon was given to carrying things in his mouth, we'd found those where nobody but he could have put them; down the clock golf hole on the lawn.

Over the years the habit had died out, however. The numbers were somewhere in the woodshed, the hole had long since filled in. Until I, hoping it might similarly interest Seeley, found the hole and cleared it out and got out the clubs.

It was more than hope. I had the feeling that if Seeley would play this game that was so personally Solomon's, it would prove there *was* a connecting link. That there was an inherited line of behaviour running through them which would make Seeley more and more like my first friend.

It was quite uncanny. One tap of the ball into the hole when the game was ready, and it was as though Solomon was with us all over again. The same exaggerated prancing after the ball; the same clowning around the hole; the same excited tearing onto the lawn when I picked up a club in the kitchen. Sheba had never been interested in clock golf; nor had Sugieh, Solomon and Sheba's mother. Was I right? One *could* get another just the same?

Now another big seal-point cat crouched by the clock golf hole while passers-by stared incredulously over the gate. 'Whass he doing then. Keeping goal?' enquired Father Adams. And then, unusually for him, who was never sentimental – 'Takes 'ee back, don't it… watching 'un,' he said.

SIXTEEN

One by one a good many things were emerging to take us back. When we first had Seeley, for instance, he'd been very scared of cars. Probably his mother had warned him to be careful of them. When one came past, anyway, even if he was safely in the garden, Seeley would crouch in terror and run indoors.

'At least we won't have that worry,' we'd said, remembering the time when Solomon only had to spot a car parked in the lane to be under it, on it – or preferably, if the owner had left a window open, inside it – before we could say Jack Robinson. And now here we were with the lighter evenings, people parking their cars to go for a stroll – and Seeley, at nine months old, as interested in motor vehicles as Solomon had been. Under them, on them – he hadn't yet found one with the window open, but he peered interestedly in through the windscreens just as Solomon had done.

'Doesn't he look like him?' I said as we sped out to get him in and to wipe the telltale footprints off yet another car. 'He does,' said Charles. 'And he acts like him, too. I only hope we have the strength to keep on running.'

Spring was now turning to early summer. You couldn't win, said Charles, coming in from his fruit trees one day. He'd kept the frost off them. He'd kept the birds off them. And now guess what? He'd gone up to see how they were doing and there was a blasted snail on one of them. Under the net, right on the top, just sticking its neck out for a shoot.

It looked like being a good crop all the same. And the weather was warm and the grass was high and Nature was absolutely abounding. Seeley was in his seventh heaven. One day Charles found him out by the stream, happily ambushing the bees. He'd discovered the spot where they came down for water and was crouched there watching them land. Another day, seeing him intently studying another part of the stream – in the long grass beside the gate – Charles investigated cautiously to see what was there... Seeley, saucer-eyed, was watching a toad. A big one, and beautifully marked, said Charles. We very rarely saw them around ourselves.

Now, too, the time was approaching for the village fête, where for the second year running Annabel had been asked to give donkey rides. We'd been a bit apprehensive the first time because she wasn't used to it, but she'd behaved herself very well. She'd given twenty-eight donkey rides and earned fourteen shillings, and only stopped dead twice. Since then, what was more, she'd been trained. A teenager in the village, who was an excellent rider herself, had taught her small sister to ride on Annabel, who was now a fully-fledged riding donkey.

They used to take her out on Saturday afternoons. At first Marian had to lead her – or perhaps tow her would be a better description, since Annabel wasn't very cooperative. But within a few weeks they were returning to say that Annabel had trotted... Annabel had cantered... and once, I regret to say, that Annabel had got down and rolled and Julie had fallen off. I watched sometimes from the window as the procession went by – Annabel marching independently ahead now, while Marian walked some way behind. Annabel was obviously imagining she was a proper horse, and Julie sat her well. There was one occasion, admittedly, when Annabel turned to the right as she was passing her stable and marched in, Julie and all – but Marian went in after them and the next moment Annabel, complete with rider, complacently reappeared.

All in all she was pretty well trained now and we weren't worrying about her behaviour at the fête at all. What we were concerned with was that she should look well-groomed and have a shining coat; Annabel's own desire being to roll in the dust and look awful.

I combed her. I brushed her. Not too hard, otherwise her coat would come right out, as we were now on the verge of summer. It wouldn't look like Annabel without her furry coat. We could start getting it out in earnest when the fête was over.

That was what we thought. I noticed her idly rubbing her back under a branch in her field one day. I must remember to saw that branch off, I told myself. Annabel liked to rub herself while she was thinking, and if we weren't careful she'd look like a poodle. Then, of course, I forgot about it, until two days later we were putting her in at night and Charles said 'Good Lord! Look at her back!' It was typical. A week to go to the fête and Annabel hadn't just rubbed the hair off in patches; she'd scrubbed herself completely raw. Not, fortunately, where her riding rug went (Annabel is too small for the smallest saddle), but right where the edge of it would come, across her withers; just where it would be particularly noticeable.

'People will think she's got mange,' said Charles despairingly. 'Honestly, you'd think she'd done it on purpose.' Perhaps she had, too, knowing Annabel; though to do her justice all animals love to scratch. Anyway, I covered the patches with boracic powder to dry them up, put talcum powder on top of that in the hope that the scent might deter the flies, and thus, having sawn off the branch so she couldn't do it again, we put her in her field next morning and awaited the inevitable comments.

'Whass the matter with she then?' enquired Father Adams, who never misses anything. 'Whass that smell round here?' demanded Fred Ferry, turning up almost simultaneously and suspiciously sniffing the air. They shook their heads sadly when I told them. 'She 'ont be givin' no old rides,' they said.

She did though. Her back was perfectly healed by Saturday, and with a tartan car rug on top of her usual one, nobody noticed the hairless bits. Thirty-five donkey rides she gave on this occasion – and I, trudging round with her, was practically on my knees.

That was that obligation over – and now, said Charles, we ought to be thinking about a holiday. He reckoned the fruit and the vegetables were just about right to leave. The nets were doing their stuff and keeping off the birds. By gosh, we were going to have some apples.

We were going to have plenty of tomatoes, too, though the peas weren't looking so bright. Field mice were getting at them and eating off all the shoots. Eventually – he didn't like doing it, but we couldn't let the crop be spoiled like that – Charles went off to buy some mousetraps. He got them in Woolworths in the nearest town and was much intrigued to see the assistant, when he asked for them, pick them up one by one from the counter and carefully examine them. 'Are some better than others?' Charles asked with interest. 'T' isn't that,' said the assistant. 'Little perishers of kids are always coming in here and setting the ruddy things. You'd never believe the times they've gone off on my fingers.'

Charles reluctantly caught a few of the marauders and then the remaining peas grew too big for mice to bother with and he was able to discard the traps. Seeley caught a few mice, too; he was quicker at it than Solomon, though he had the same capacity for letting them get away. Sheba had been a tremendous mouser in her time, but she didn't bother with it much now, so we were most intrigued by her behaviour one morning. Seeley had caught a shrew – and, to my relief, had promptly lost it, so I didn't have to go to the rescue. Sheba sat languidly by, apparently not even looking. That was for Children; her mousing days were Past; she couldn't be bothered with such Trivia, her expression implied. I was absolutely amazed, therefore, when Charles came in a while later and said that Sheba, who hadn't been outside the gate in ages, was out in the lane with Seeley and they were watching for mice side by side. 'What on earth do you think that's in aid of?' I said. 'He's probably told her that he keeps losing them,' said Charles. 'And she's got him out there giving him a lesson.'

They were certainly fond of one another. Whenever Seeley, returning from one of his expeditions, went running up to

156

her with his 'Mrr-mrr-mrrr' of greeting, Sheba would give him a deeper 'Mrrr-mrr' back. She was still his Number One pin-up girl, too. Often, when they sat together, he'd give a lick behind her ears like a doting parent tidying a child's hair, and then he'd look at us most proudly. Not bad, Was She? he was obviously asking.

We learned how much she really meant to him, though, the day I put him in his cage on his own. They'd been going in there together daily for about six weeks without any fuss. Indeed, it worked so well that Sugar and Spice's owners had now put up a similar cage for them. That greyhound came to visit so often, they said, they couldn't stand the strain.

This was one of Sheba's off-days, however. She didn't fancy her breakfast. She wanted to sleep on our bed. So we decided to let her stay there and, as it was a sunny day and it seemed a shame to keep him indoors, to put Seeley in the cage on his own. Immediately he was in there he began to howl. 'Because Sheba isn't with him,' I said. 'When I've finished these letters I'll let him out and keep an eye on him.' By the time I'd done the letters, however, Seeley had let himself out. Unable to get through the laced-up corners, he climbed the wire and, while clinging to one of the front support poles, had chewed a hole clean through what was supposed to be an unbreakable nylon net. Very intelligently done it was, too, with every thread that mattered chewed in a determinedly straight line.

Now he'd discovered how to do that, I said, we'd have to put the cage up permanently, with a proper wire roof. We didn't, though. Next day Sheba was her normal self so, pressed for time as usual, I mended the hole with string, put them both in there temporarily, expecting Seeley to chew through the net within minutes – and he just didn't bother. He simply sunned himself happily there with Sheba, occasionally rolling on the rug or getting up to swat a fly, as if the idea of escape had never entered his head. And now – if, as she often does, Sheba goes into the cage voluntarily (it being sheltered in there and strategically placed to catch the sun), Seeley is usually right behind her. Just as, in bygone days, Solomon would have been.

They make a happy picture together, and there is no doubt that he has done her tremendous good. Without him we would probably have lost her – instead of which a few weeks back, for the first time in years, Sheba rushed skittishly up the damson tree. We had to fetch the ladder to get her down, but not on account of her age. It was midnight and, sitting up there talking to us, Sheba would have tantalised us for hours.

She could climb better than Seeley could, Couldn't She? (I'll say she could. She was right at the very top.) It was Difficult getting up to her, wasn't it? (It certainly was, on a dark night with a torch.) She'd made us give her lots of Attention, hadn't she? demanded Sheba when we finally got her down. And indoors, watching frustratedly from the window, sat Seeley. Wanted to be up the Tree with Sheba! he bawled.

Well, that was really something, said Charles as we carried her in. Who'd ever have thought we'd see her act like that again? She was good for a good few years yet, he reckoned... Which reminded him, what about fixing up that holiday? We'd better ring the Francises and find out when they could take the cats. He bet they'd be looking forward to meeting Seeley.

Annabel was going to our local farm, where she'd stayed when we were on holiday ever since we'd had her. That marked the passing of the years with us, too... from the time when she was so tiny they'd fenced her off from the cows and she'd crawled indignantly under the barrier and put the herd to flight. There was the year they'd put her in with the heifers... the year they'd put her in with the older cows... The previous year had marked Annabel's supremacy, when we'd come back and found her in charge of the bull. 'Call her from the gate, mind,' said Mrs Pursey when we went to fetch her. 'William's pretty docile, but it's always best to be sure.'

William is another character. Earlier that spring he'd been out in the field adjoining the road with his wives and, as Farmer Pursey believed in locking him in every night for safety (not that William was dangerous but some fool might let him out), one of the features of the local scene had been Farmer Pursey calling him at about five o'clock every evening and waving a mangold, and William, who loves mangolds as dearly as Seeley loves turkey, sprinting across the field and following anticipatorily through the gate, across the road and down to his shed in the farmyard.

One Saturday afternoon, however, Farmer Pursey went to a football match and wasn't back by five o'clock. William waited and waited and waited. After about twenty minutes the bellows of a bull urgently demanding his mangold began to rend the air. We heard the noise down in the Valley and wondered whatever it was. And finally William, refusing to wait any longer, broke through the hedge. Not, fortunately, into the road, but into a neighbouring garden where, when Farmer Pursey returned a short while later, William was still snorting and loudly demanding his mangold while the owners of the bungalow kept watch on him – not from any fear of his fierceness, but so that he shouldn't run away.

This being William, it was no surprise to us when we went to the gate and saw him grazing meekly in the field with Annabel in full command. She was only about half as tall as he was but there she stood, queening it over him and a cow and two calves like Cleopatra in the land of Egypt. It was a good thing we didn't go into the field, at that. He followed her right to the gate.

What she'd get up to this year, goodness only knew. There was a new Scotch collie for her to play with, and Mrs Pursey always spoiled her. What Seeley would get up to at Halstock we didn't know either, and we certainly weren't looking forward to the journey. Howling all the way, said Charles, shuddering at the very thought. But he bet he'd like it when he got there... Remember the first time Solomon and Sheba went there as kittens, he said, and they'd liked the earthbox so much they'd gone to sleep in it?

I remembered. I remembered so many things. We were right in having Seeley. He has been good for Sheba. He has been good for us. The household is normal once more. Even as I have finished this book I have seen something I never expected to see again. Seeley and Sheba sitting side by side in the kitchen, their tails affectionately crossed.

If, sometimes, I look across to where the daffodils are and say 'Oh, Solomon... Solomon... Solomon...'... nobody ever hears me. I whisper it to myself.